P9-BIW-920

The Growth of Early Old World Civilizations, *Robert M. Adams*

The Stages of Human Evolution: Human and Cultural Origins, *C. Loring Brace*

The Sub-Human Primates and Their Social Life, *Michael R. A. Chance and Clifford J. Jolly*

New World Prehistory: Archaeology of the American Indian, *William T. Sanders and Joseph J. Marino*

Linguistic Anthropology, *A. Richard Diebold, Jr.*

Ethnological Theory, *David Kaplan*

Formation of the State, *Lawrence Krader*

Tribesmen, *Marshall D. Sahlins*

The Hunters, *Elman R. Service*

Peasants, *Eric R. Wolf*

The Present as Anthropology, *Peter Worsley*

The Evolutionary Basis of Race, *Ernst Goldschmidt*

FOUNDATIONS OF MODERN ANTHROPOLOGY SERIES

Marshall D. Sahlins, *Editor*

FOUNDATIONS OF MODERN ANTHROPOLOGY SERIES

PRENTICE-HALL, INC., Englewood Cliffs, New Jersey

Lawrence Krader, City University of New York

Formation

of the State

© Copyright 1968 by PRENTICE-HALL, INC., Englewood Cliffs, New Jersey.

All rights reserved. No part of this book may be reproduced

in any form by any means without permission

in writing from the publisher. Printed in the United States of America.

Library of Congress Catalog Card No. 68–10655.

Designed by Harry Rinehart.

PRENTICE-HALL

FOUNDATIONS OF MODERN ANTHROPOLOGY SERIES

Marshall D. Sahlins, *Editor*

Current printing (last digit):
10 9 8 7 6 5 4 3 2 1

PRENTICE-HALL INTERNATIONAL, INC., *London*
PRENTICE-HALL OF AUSTRALIA, PTY., LTD., *Sydney*
PRENTICE-HALL OF CANADA, LTD., *Toronto*
PRENTICE-HALL OF INDIA PVT. LTD., *New Delhi*
PRENTICE-HALL OF JAPAN, INC., *Tokyo*

Foundations

of Modern Anthropology

Series

The Foundations of Modern Anthropology Series is a documentation of the human condition, past and present. It is concerned mainly with exotic peoples, prehistoric times, unwritten languages, and unlikely customs. But this is merely the anthropologist's way of expressing his concern for the here and now, and his way makes a unique contribution to our knowledge of what's going on in the world. We cannot understand ourselves apart from an understanding of *man*, nor our culture apart from an understanding of *culture*. Inevitably we are impelled toward an intellectual encounter with man in all his varieties, no matter how primitive, how ancient, or how seemingly insignificant. Ever since their discovery by an expanding European civilization, primitive peoples have continued to hover over thoughtful men like ancestral ghosts, ever provoking this anthropological curiosity. To "return to the primitive" just for what it is would be foolish; the savage is not nature's nobleman and his existence is no halcyon idyll. For anthropology, the romance of the primitive has been something else:

a search for the roots and meaning of ourselves—in the context of all mankind.

The series, then, is designed to display the varieties of man and culture and the evolution of man and culture. All fields of anthropology are relevant to the grand design and all of them—prehistoric archaeology, physical anthropology, linguistics, and ethnology (cultural anthropology)—are represented among the authors of the several books in the series. In the area of physical anthropology are books describing the early condition of humanity and the subhuman primate antecedents. The later development of man on the biological side is set out in the volume on races, while the archaeological accounts of the Old World and the New document development on the historical side. Then there are the studies of contemporary culture, including a book on how to understand it all—i.e., on ethnological theory—and one on language, the peculiar human gift responsible for it all. Main types of culture are laid out in "The Hunters," "Tribesmen," "Formation of the State," and "Peasants." Initiating a dialogue between contemplation of the primitive and the present, the volume on "The Present as Anthropology" keeps faith with the promise of anthropological study stated long ago by E. B. Tylor, who saw in it "the means of understanding our own lives and our place in the world, vaguely and imperfectly it is true, but at any rate more clearly than any former generation."

Preface

This book is concerned with formation of the state. The word "formation" may be understood in one of two ways: either as the coming into being of the state—that is to say, how it was formed; or again, as the resultant formation—that is, the finished product. Our usage is primarily the first, the emphasis being on the process of formation. To be sure, there is an interaction between the process of formation and the result, the state being an on-going process of formation of an institution. It is by no means a finished product, at least through the foreseeable future. Man will have to live under a system of states for some time to come; hopeful people of the last century, who foresaw the withering away of the state, are seen as too optimistic, for the moment.

The institution, it should be stressed, is a social institution, a product of human society. It arose out of social conditions, which are set forth in the text. It is not a metaphysical abstraction as the late philosopher Jacques Maritain and others before him maintained. In order to show what the state is and what it is not, these various views will be discussed.

The state is a political institution, which we define as an institution of government. As such, it exists alongside, and in interrelation with, other institutions of human society. However, it is not the only political institution, for there are other ways of governing a society than by means of the state. These alternative modes of government, which are found among certain primitive peoples, are described below. The transition from government without the state through intermediate forms leading to the formation of the state are next taken up, in which greater complexity of social and economic life are found. Here societies increase in size and productive power; ritual kings begin to make their appearance.

The book ranges over space and time, to show the build-up of greater and greater institutions of economy, government, religion, and society, until the state properly so-called appears, in ancient Egypt and elsewhere, answering to the criteria for the formation of the state which we established at the outset.

This book, then, has a thesis: there is such a thing as the political state, which is found only in certain societies. It has a role in these societies that is uniform throughout, controlling and directing the life of the people under it by centralized social power in the hands of a few. Certain anthropologists, who are discussed at the beginning and at the end of the book, maintain that the state is found everywhere in human society, under all social conditions. Other anthropologists maintain that the state is an unnecessary concept in social analysis, since terms such as government will do, and have already been introduced. If our conceptual scheme proves correct, then these other views will have to be set aside.

The thesis is advanced in the study of a few selected peoples who appeared to me to exhibit one important factor above all, the increasing complexity of state formation, in relation to the increasing complexity of social and economic life. The method employed has called for setting the political factor in the broader social context, therefore, and I have sought in every case to do so. I have dealt with only a few societies which instance this developmental relationship, and have focused, necessarily, only on these few aspects of the broader problem of state formation.

The works of political scientists, philosophers, sociologists, and historians, together with anthropologists, have all contributed to the development of the notion of the state. I suggest that, beginning with this field (which—as the editor of the series, Dr. Marshall Sahlins, has proposed—belongs to the Foundations of Anthropology), the student branch out into the related literature. Perhaps, therefore, the Selected References are the most important part of the book.

My own work has been concentrated, as far as the materials in this book are concerned, on the peoples discussed in the latter part, the Mongols and the Slavs. It is not, however, the peoples that I have to bring to the attention of the reader, but the peoples in relation to what is here our main problem. Thereby I hope to provide some insight into the fateful instrumentality of concentrated political power.

A number of years ago, Dr. Paul Kirchhoff, now of Mexico, set me to thinking about this problem in an anthropological way. Dr. Robert M. Adams, of the University of Chicago, whose specialty is the ancient Middle East, has given generously of his time and knowledge. My thanks go to them, and to Mr. W. Mangas, of the Project Planning Department of Prentice-Hall, for his concern for my prose. Naturally, the responsibility for what follows rests only with myself.

Lawrence Krader

Contents

Introduction

Inquiry into the nature and origins of the state has been a traditional concern of cultural anthropology. Precursors of anthropological thought—Jean Jacques Rousseau, Adam Ferguson, Condorcet—took up the problem in the eighteenth century. These men were reformers and revolutionists who considered that civilization should be made more perfect, that the agency of change was political action, and that politics was located in government and the state. The aims of a more perfect society were then much as they are today: all people under the law should be equal before it, without special privileges or rights, and therefore rights should be general; all people should have freedom within the limits of the law, so long as they keep within those limits; and finally, the law should reflect the customs of the people and not depart from them in a radical and arbitrary manner (for example, if it is a custom to keep dogs as pets, no state law should be created which will rule this out)—that is, the law should not come into conflict with custom unless custom itself interferes with equality of right and freedom.

1

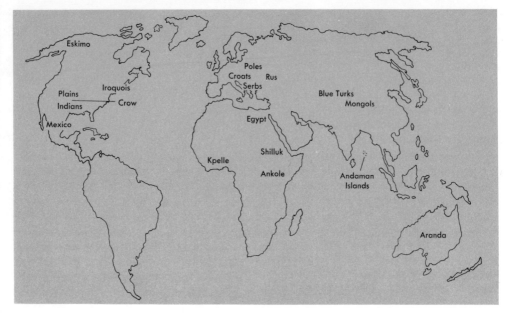

Major locations of peoples who formed the states.

State and Society

The eighteenth-century thinkers worked on a series of assumptions: that a society such as the American and its form of government by the state were bound together inseparably; that both could be made more perfect; and hence that progress of society and progress of the state were one and the same. In the nineteenth century, optimism concerning the future of man continued to prevail, but there was a change in tone. Eighteenth-century optimism was based on legislative reform, conscious political judgment, and action. Revolution was the servant of the legislature and the legislature was the rational servant of the people. However, in the following century, humanity was considered to be subject to involuntary forces—either swift and revolutionary forces, or slow and evolutionary forces, or a combination of the two—leading inevitably in the direction of progress. In the nineteenth century, certain anthropologists continued to hold that society and the state were everywhere found together; that there was no human society without the state. Some anthropologists hold this view today. But the consideration of society *without* the state had already been introduced in the nineteenth century, and this is the view which will be advanced here.

Lewis H. Morgan, writing in the nineteenth century on the growth of the idea of government among the Iroquois, Aztecs, Greeks, and Romans, began the investigation of the origin of the state in its modern form. Today we conceive that the state has a central place in the account of the development of society. The state is not a monster; neither is it the perfect instrument for the achievement of human aims. Rather, the state has developed as mankind has developed: from simple beginnings to ever more complicated and formal social structures. Simple peoples, consisting of families or groups of families, were grouped in the consanguineal order of society, wherein kinship is the dominant bond between tribesmen. The civil plan of society, again, as

2

Morgan put it, is found among the complex societies which appear later in time. Therefore, a progression from one stage to another is to be inferred.

During the 1920's and 1930's, Robert Lowie, Robert MacIver, and Richard Thurnwald continued work on the origin and development of the state. Lowie regarded the state as having developed out of the *association,* a grouping of people within a society for limited purposes, which cuts across local community and kinship ties, combining individual members into this new social grouping. The state, he wrote, is not found everywhere in human society in full-fledged form. It is a germ or potentiality in all societies, realized in some of them. To form a state, people have to be pulled together from many local communities in which they live; they must be torn out of local context and brought together under a different sort of organization. The association is one means (among many) of doing this. Lowie examined the Crow Indian association, which policed their buffalo hunt in the western Plains, as one which potentially forms the state. Thurnwald, on the other hand, conceived the state to be formed by the conquest of one people by another. In doing so, he brought forward a theory which had been severely criticized, and has since had to be modified. But Thurnwald added a psychological factor based on the East African example, as we shall see.

The state is to be defined in terms of the size and relative complexity of the society in which it is found, and in the nature of the authority within the society. The state is the means of governing societies with large populations numbering many thousands or millions, and is found only in such societies. The state is found only in societies with numerous composite groups, social classes, and associations, bringing together under common rule many kinds of people; a society having a state form of government is not usually ethnically homogeneous. Such a society is divided into social classes and strata; it is unequal in the distribution of economic functions and of wealth. States bring together the different classes and communities under common rule. Authority in *any* form of state issues from one central office and is usually asserted impersonally and objectively, in the name of a god, or the majesty of the throne, or the people. Now there are means of conducting human affairs in formal offices and institutions of rule with specialized assignments of roles to governors of provinces, judges, soldiers, kings, ministers, police; or by informal assignments of these roles. People on occasion act as judges, ministers, soldiers in simple societies. But differences in population size and complexity, and formality of office, make for radical differences in modes of government; the larger, more complex and formal governmental roles are usually found in states. The state is a complicating factor in the organization of society, a factor that works two ways: on the one hand, its presence is the mark that a complex form *has been achieved;* on the other, the process of forming the state is a means for *achieving the transition to* complex society. That is, a more complex society is established by the process of state formation.

Unity and Diversity of the State

The emergence and formation of the state will be considered as a complex of processes, since the state was developed in many places and times and under varying conditions, and the social formation which thus emerged has many variants. In what sense then may we discuss the *state*, and in what sense *states*? There have been and are city-states, empire-states, theocratic states, tribal-consanguineal states, nation-states, centralized states, and decentralized states; autocratic, oligarchic, and democratic states; states stratified by class, caste, and social estate. At one time under Fascism there was, and perhaps today there still is, mention made of corporate states. It is possible to trace the development of these state forms separately. Alternatively, one may begin with the state as we know it in all the countries of the modern world. The governing of modern nations has a structure and functioning in common to warrant the common name of state. But following the idea of plurality of formations as set forth above, we must further ask: In which types of societies, where, and how far back in time, may we trace the general form?

Although states have taken many forms, they all exhibit certain common features. These features, even under diverse origins and circumstances, emerge from the answers the state provides to the same repeated questions concerning the governing of large and complex groups of people.

Of the various types of states, noted above, many have disappeared or are disappearing—for instance, the *city-states*, found in ancient, medieval, and Renaissance periods. Judging by size of territory and population, these were small states even for their time, as compared with the Egyptian, Persian, Roman, or Chinese empires, and were established around a city, such as Ur of Chaldaea in southern Mesopotamia, Athens in ancient Greece, or Venice in medieval and Renaissance times. They conducted their own foreign affairs, regulated their internal lives, engaged in commerce and manufacture and served as the cult centers of their territories. Other states have controlled great empires—so-called "mother countries" with dependent populations and territories. These too have virtually disappeared, or have been so reduced in size that today there are few dependent populations and territories. There were likewise at one time tribes having internal political organization sufficiently complex and tight to be known as *tribe-states*. They are smaller on the average than states usually are, and the political offices within them usually have fewer formal roles than are found in states. Although the term "tribal state" was applied by Bronislaw Malinowski, an anthropologist of the past generation, it has not been used in this volume because the distinction from other types of state is too vague. In any case, most have since been formed into modern states or have disappeared.

There have been states in the past, such as the state in medieval times in Mongolia, which had ill-defined territorial limits, whose subjects were related to one another by ties of kinship—hence a kind of *consanguineal state*, which no longer exists. States today have fixed territorial limits; citizenship is established in their territories by right of having been born in the land or descended from parents born in the land or having been naturalized so that one can live there, enjoying rights and obligations as though one had been born there. These are *nation-states*. The nation-state was developed in Europe at the end of the medieval period and beginning of modern times; today it is the dominant form of the state in almost every part of the world. It has been established in the Americas, Asia, Africa. It has been adapted to many forms of political ideology, some of which, such as the Socialist and Communist, had not even been conceived at the time that the form of the nation-state was first established.

The historical trend has been to reduce the number of state forms to one predominant form—the nation-state—by a process of cultural diffusion from Europe to other parts of the world; during this process contact among peoples has occurred. This form was then combined with indigenous systems of political rule in a number of variations: one-party systems, many-party systems, parliamentary, autarchic, or oligarchic rule, and so forth.

The unity of the nation-state today is based not on common ancestry, or on ethnic or cultural unity, but rather on unity in a polity over a territory. Peoples making up the nation are usually of different origins, as in the United States. A national culture arises, based on shared experiences and concerns; shared institutions, goals, and symbols; a common language (or failing that, or in addition to it, a unified communications system by means of newspapers, television, radio, schools, posters). Most nations have a single national language, but a few, such as Belgium, Canada, India, the Soviet Union, and Switzerland, have more than one, with consequent problems of political and linguistic adjustment. Some multilingual nations, such as Switzerland with its four official languages (French, German, Italian, and Romansch), have adjusted better than others to their internal composite life.

Formerly, states were formed in many parts of the world, independently of one another, as parallel developments. Today, however, culture contact, or *acculturation*, is ever more intensive, and parallel development, corollary with isolated development, is less common.

All states share certain problems: regulating and making secure the lives of citizens and residents of each; regulating and adjusting relations between states; seeing to the welfare of members of one state who live under the laws of another state. Modern states have diplomatic and consular services, levy taxes and duties, nurture those in need, provide for public education, and strictly delimit and defend their borders. Such states tend to adopt similar solutions to problems of internal regulation and external relations, and hence to resemble each other ever more closely.

The number of forms which states have taken is being reduced both by external factors of diffusion and culture contact, and by internal and systematic factors arising out of functions operating within all states and out of common problems to be solved. In recent decades, new nations of Africa, Asia, and the Indo-Pacific island world have been formed, older nations in these areas and in the Americas and Europe have been reformed, and new sets of relationships among states and peoples have been introduced. The European form of the nation-state has been re-adapted to new conditions, both with changes and recognizable continuity of form and function, in other parts of the world.

There are yet other questions to be considered in studying the state: In what sense does Roman, Mongol, or French society coincide with the state of the Roman or Mongol Empires or of the French Republic? Can society and state, and government and state, be considered the same? Is the state found everywhere in human society, or is it characteristic only of certain types of society? Is there a single, predominating definition of the term "state," governing all its different forms?

If you would know what a state is, look around you. The world is divided into sharply defined political units, the boundaries of which are the subject of unceasing concern: international negotiations, military defense. The piercing of these boundaries without express consent of the indigenous authorities may be a cause of war. Within these boundaries there is a sovereign authority which is, in theory at least, self-sufficient and self-dependent. That is, the state as a self-governing body answers to none, whatever its past history may have been, or however its power may be derived. This is a myth, of course: states are answerable to comities of states; but citizens and subjects have no recourse other than to constituted authorities within their state. Moreover, the state is self-venerating, making a cult of its territorial integrity, political independence, and all-powerful authority within the area and scope of its sovereign rule. The chiefs of state today are presidents, premiers, and kings, surrounded by civil and military councilors and police agents. The public, subjects and citizenry, cannot approach these rulers on ceremonial occasions, such as a coronation or an inauguration, and can only approach them on invitation or through proper channels at other times. The rulers within their domains summon, they are never summoned. These supreme offices are both pompous and powerful, expressing and embodying the sovereign power of the states which they run.

However, this was not always so. Archaeological evidence indicates no great ceremonial centers or great courts until the rise of the empires of Egypt, China, and Mexico within the last 6,000 years. Before that time men lived more simply, if the material remains of those times are reliable indexes. Many tribes today are lacking in the great centers of ceremony and of might; their tribesmen live quite simply, and if they have a chief at all, they can approach him without circumstance or special effort.

Plan of the Book

In this book, the order of presentation of societies will be according to the relative complexity of their governmental arrangements. First, the simplest societies will be taken up: those having a government, but one which is not organized in the form of a state. Then we will consider societies still lacking the state but in which certain institutions also found in more stable and complex form in the state (an association for police or religious functions, and central offices of cult or rule) have developed modestly. Next, societies with simple forms of the state will be discussed. Finally, civilizations with a complex and definitive realization of the state in all its forms and functions will be examined. Notice that all societies have some form of government (that is, ways of internally ordering their social affairs), but that not all societies achieve this condition by means of the state form of rulership.

Typology of the State

Simple Societies without the State

Eskimos, Bushmen, Pygmies all have governments of a sort. The Eskimo example will serve in this book to cover the type of government lacking the state. The Eskimos live in bands numbering a few score or at most a few hundred members. These bands run their own affairs, organize subsistence hunting and fishing, and deal as equals with their neighbors. Each band has a territory of its own, moving the site of residence from place to place within the territory, and adding or losing families accordingly as the life necessities within their territory are rich or poor at any given time.

Societies with Institutions Leading to the State

Societies with a stabler economy and stabler social life in village settlements also have a more constant population size and a more complex social organization. One such society was that of the Crow Indians who inhabited the Great Plains in western North America in the last century; their village formation was more settled in place of residence and population size than that of the Eskimo band. The Crow had an organization which policed their buffalo hunt, a major activity providing for much of their subsistence. Although this organization, which punished infractions of rules of the hunt, was situational (that is, it did not function outside the hunting situation), it was the germ of the kind of institution that grows into the full-blown state.

The Kpelle are farmers of Liberia, West Africa, who observed a centralized rule of sorts: a dual center of power. The Shilluk—cattle-raisers who live in the upper portion of the Sudan in the Nile Valley—practiced a cult of the divine king, who reigned but did not rule. Both Kpelle and Shilluk, embracing much larger populations than Eskimo bands have, live in relative stability in stationary village groupings which do not readily grow or shrink. Whereas the Kpelle social order maintained (though only equivocally) the center of power (the kingship) over the subjects, the Shilluk (because the royal institution lacked ultimate coercive authority) instead merely represented by means of symbolic ritual the unity of the people in and under the office of the king. This is in all likelihood still the case with the Shilluk, although we report here only their situation of a generation ago.

Just as the nineteenth-century Crow were, the Kpelle and Shilluk are state-less societies; yet—like the Crow—their institutions, taken together, to a marked degree contain the ideas and practices germinal to state formation. The Crow, Shilluk, and Kpelle police and royal institutions, which have compelled the obedience or engaged the loyalty of the members of the community and of the society, should be regarded as necessary but not sufficient conditions for the formation of the state; they are halfway houses which exhibit features of government and social organization found in the state.

There are profound differences in method of rule between Crow or Kpelle political life and that of states. The central power of government is more fully developed in the state than it is in the Kpelle kind of polity, and the state power is more fully articulated—that is, is divided into functioning parts and assigned to different offices and ministries, each with its area of competence: councils, cult and war offices, and so on. These offices or ministries tend to act throughout the territory of the state, and do not live well with isolated and independent centers of power which are only in theory subordinate. The decrees and laws of the central power are, or should be, universal throughout the land. Only in the state form of political organization have universal rights and laws been developed.

The Ankole kingdom of East Africa formed a modest and simple state when the tradition was still alive, a mere one generation ago. This state was formed by conquest. Since the theory of the conquest state is a prominent one, the discussion of Ankole will be introduced by a brief account of conquest theory and the controversy surrounding it.

In its day, the Ankole polity was larger than most of the societies already mentioned, composed as it was of distinct economic elements: farmers, herdsmen, traders, and the like. (Eskimo, Crow, Kpelle, and Shilluk societies are homogeneous, every community living much as the next one.) These elements of the Ankole polity were partly, though not fully, integrated into an economic whole, under a kingship—a central authority and supreme sovereignty which was the object of a royal cult and which possessed a workable degree of delegated power. Its community life was stable, and it was (and still is) a society of complex composition. Its borders were dominated by border chiefs who operated with a high degree of independence. (The conquerors had not entirely mastered the conquered, nor had they fully mastered the territory over which they ruled.) Because limitations on state formation came from the lack of a fully unifying integration of different parts of the polity and economy, Ankole is called an *emergent state*.

The State Properly So-called

The states of ancient Egypt, of medieval Russia, and of Tatary, were fully formed state-empires, or *empire-states*. They were all of great size, whether measured against Ankole or Kpelle, or even against modern nation-states. The vast society of the Mongol Empire which developed in medieval Tatary included in its ranks hundreds of thousands of soldiers, just as did the societies of the Rus of Kiev and Egypt. They each had a stable village life, although this was and is nomadic in the case of the Mongols, their nomadism having a predictable procedure and structure. The Mongols had only one predominant source of livelihood, their herds; but the winning of this livelihood was related to dealing in trade with the agricultural products of neighboring China by a marketing and exchange system (which will be discussed presently).

The beginnings of state rule and structure may be traced among Egyptians, Slavs, and Mongols. There are accounts of these peoples which indicate that at first they did not live under state domination, but only in their later history came under the rule of kings, ministers, generals—in short, under a state form of rule. How they made the transition from one way of life to the other will be described in the latter part of this book.

The rise of the state in Egypt of the pharaohs is a case of state religion, royal cult, and god-king. Ancient Egypt formed a state in which religion served a double purpose. Émile Durkheim showed that a religion is the representation of the unity of the people who profess it, and thus, that a primary role of religion is as cultural unifier. But the state religion in Egypt, as elsewhere, served a secondary purpose: to unify the people under the monarchy. Again, the Mongol state was formed under its emperor, who brought his people together under the imperial office. The procedure followed was in two steps, showing the working-out in detail of this theory of religion and the state.

In the cases of Egyptians, Mongols, and Slavs, the state was first formed by internal expansion and internal conquest. Mongols first conquered their neighbors who were Mongols, and other pastoral nomads of Asia. They then embarked on broader conquests. Russians and other Slavs likewise affirmed the area of central rule first within their areas and then without. Thus, stratification of society, internal and external conquest, and integration of communities into larger wholes, went hand-in-hand. In integrating diverse communities within a common polity, different functions were introduced: specialized police, tax collectors, governors, military leaders, clergy. These innovations formed a specialized ruling strata which went hand-in-hand with increasing specialization of function elsewhere in society. Unlike Ankole, these states underwent considerable political and economic development before the formations for which they are historically known. They also show the beginnings of internal stratification before the great conquests; there is no evidence that Ankole participated in such processes.

In a purely formal way, Ankole was a less well-developed state as compared with the Egyptian or Mongol empires. The concentration of power in Egypt and Mongolia proceeded by a ritual whereby political power was formally delegated by the people to the kingly office. The king then delegated the power thus concentrated in ministries and offices.

Our fundamental conclusion is that although political activity and organization is found everywhere in human society, the government of men is not always and everywhere organized in permanent institutions of the state. There are, to be sure, governments with such central and permanent institutions as kingship, but they lack the social and economic developments found in other societies ruled by states; and without the supporting governmental apparatus of the state, such institutions are weak and often purely formal.

In the organization of the state, man concentrates his power over man in a single office. The monopoly of physical force by this office is absolute. It may channel its power by specifically delegating it; otherwise, unless the state is overthrown, the power remains at the disposal of the central authority. The force in the hands of the state takes various forms: banishment, death, imprisonment, enslavement, fines. But the forces of the state are not merely negative. The state draws upon the integrative forces of society: love, loyalty, mutual dependence, religious faith, tradition, and inertia.

Further, the state is a central authority (kingship, presidency) over people within a fixed territory. But it is more than a physical, territorial, legal unity: the central office transforms national unity, representation, defense, and control of that unity into an ideology. The invasion of the territory of a state is doubly a threat: invasion diminishes the geographic area of the state, and hence diminishes the scope of the central authority, reducing the power it enjoys. The ideology of unity of state and territory, of state and people in society, is endangered together with its physical extent. Loyalty to the state is founded, in part, on acceptance of its power and belief in it. Weakness can be a threat to this faith; or it may be that weakness will attract greater devotion than ever. But in either case the populace responds to the state and its destiny, not merely to loss of population, territory, or wealth.

All societies have rules of behavior, and punish infractions of those rules. Some societies have measures which not only punish the rule-breakers but also limit the recurrence of infractions. But law- and rule-breaking in the state not only may injure the person and property of a member of the society, but also may diminish and threaten the central power and the system of law and order administered by the central power. The essential difference between the state and other political forms is this: the state has its own mystique of power, which is *superadded*; the state is in this sense a secondary formation. Just as maintenance of internal order and defense have a double meaning in the state (regulation and defense of the society and of the state itself), so social integration has a double meaning (integration of society under state domination). Religion expresses the sense of collectivity of the society; state religion is the expression of the integration of the society within and under the supreme power.

The state is found only in large and complex societies and economies. As the central authority in these societies, it is a secondary formation in every case. In all societies of mankind, government and politics are the means of maintaining internal order and external defense, and of representing to themselves and to others the unity of the people. The state performs all these tasks, just as societies without the state do, but the state also acts on its own behalf, seeking by identifying with the society over which it rules to advance its rulership. The state is not an independent thing, but is the institution of society in which the political power is concentrated and monopolized.

One *An Anthropological Theory of the State*

Robert Lowie wrote *The Origin of the State* in 1926, starting from the premises that all of mankind had and has the same kind of mentality, and that peoples differ only in the ways of expressing that mentality. This common mentality, or psychic unity of mankind, was connected by Lowie to the concept of a continuous story of man. Everywhere the same physical and social problems of man are met by cultural means, varying according to the different peoples on earth. Among the problems is that of internally ordering social life. He proposed that the complexity of social life organized under a state form of rule could be traced back to a simple origin, an institution which contained the seed which then flowered into the fully formed state. People living in simple communities, villages, bands, or clans organized ways of relating to each other by means of local ties such as the village, and kinship ties such as the clan. But in order to build the state they had to be related in more extensive groupings reaching beyond the locality or the kindred—in a word, through the *association*. Lowie did not argue that the state is to be found everywhere in human society; what he said was that the association is an institution which may be found in societies without the state, and that it is by the further development of this institution that the state is formed.

Through the association the continuity of man's social life may be traced from the most primitive condition to the most complex.

Cultural Continuities
and Discontinuities

Cultural Continuities

Eduard Meyer, historian of ancient society, and Wilhelm Koppers, modern ethnologist, went further: they held the state to be a universal element in human social organization. Meyer's view was many-sided: If the state is defined as the organizing and unifying principle in all social organization of mankind, then in that sense the state is omnipresent in human society. However, he also analyzed the state as a complex and sophisticated system of political rule, such as was found in the high cultures of the ancient Near East. In his history of ancient Egypt, the state was represented only in the dynastic period, at the end of the fourth millennium B.C., and not prior to that epoch.

Aristotle, an initiator of this line of inquiry in general, wrote that man by his nature is a *political* animal (political is taken to mean *civilized*, perhaps in the modern anthropological sense, and also *cultured*). Man lives in close relationship with other men, as in cities. Aristotle's *zoon politikon*, "political animal," means "one living in cities or in like places," for the Greek term *polis* means "city, city-state," forming the root for the word "political" hence, "of the city." In English we maintain the Latin tradition which equated Greek *polis* with Latin *civis*, which in turn serves as the root for "city, civilized." Now Aristotle's conception went beyond the reference to urban man, and referred to the interdependent nature of man in close settlement, urban or rural. There are no isolated men; society is universal in the life of mankind. But only certain kinds of men are civilized; this great political enterprise, according to Aristotle, is in the nature of mankind, which is fully realized only in the civilized condition: this concept is "political," related in a sense to ours, and includes among other things the governing of men.

Cultural Discontinuities

Continuity pairs with discontinuity. Certain aspects of culture, such as government, are universal; others, such as the state, are not. Human societies may be grouped in two categories, according to whether they share features of social organization which have gone into the formation of the state. We oppose the view that the state is found universally in human society; we propose instead that the presence or absence of the state among a given people places that people in one or another of the two categories. The presence of the state is the mark of discontinuity in cultural development, for societies with the state differ from each other in degree, but differ in kind from societies without the state. But the factor of the state is not only a dividing line between two levels of human development, it is also by its formation the means of straddling and crossing the line.

Definition of the State

The state is a non-primitive form of government. Unlike primitive forms of government, the agencies of government by the state are usually explicit, complex, and formal. Although the complex institutions of the state help to integrate the society out of which it arises, human society has other means of composing its integration than the state. Integration is accomplished positively: (1) by expression, in a ritualistic and formal way, of the unity of the society (this is done in societies with and without the state); (2) by an ideological expression, in which the society as a whole, and its agency, the state, are glorified and venerated; (3) by securing the internal peace of the society; (4) by protection of its external borders; and (5) by pursuing foreign relations advantageous to itself and to the people it rules. Integration is accomplished negatively by suppression of disruptive acts of crime, terror, rebellion. The central authority delegates the integrative powers involved in these activities to foreign ministries, war ministries, the police, etc., as the case may be. The state integrates the society which it rules in a manner different from that whereby a society without the state achieves its internal integration. Government is one of the means whereby integration is assured, and government differs between societies with and without the state.

The State, Society, and Political Behavior

The state has been made into an object of reverence both for its intellectual appeal and for its brute, coercive force. J. Maritain has considered the state to be the ideal and practical embodiment of the human quintessence, the rational order of society; Hegel regarded the state as the realization of the ethical idea in society. But others have worshiped the state because it concentrates all physical force in one hand which might be delivered up to them.

The state has been endowed by some with a will, as though it were a human being. But it is inadmissible to regard the state or any other social collectivity as a biological organism with a will of its own; this is the error into which such social philosophers as August Schaeffle and Herbert Spencer fell in the nineteenth century. A. L. Kroeber suggested the term "superorganic" to characterize human society and culture, in order to avoid the analogy of society to an organism, and at the same time to bring out the collective nature of social life.

J. Bluntschli, a nineteenth-century political philosopher, qualified the will of the state as a "collective will" as opposed to an "individual will," and in so doing differentiated between the social whole and the biological organism.

But the collective will is the idealization of ill-defined processes of political action, whether by consensus or by dictation; the collective will is a figure of speech.

The difference between society and the state was discussed at length by Bluntschli. From the time of Rousseau until the end of the nineteenth century, French political theory had regarded the state and society as one. To the contrary, Bluntschli maintained that while the state is organized with a head and members, society is not. Society has neither collective will nor political power, legislation, government, or administration of justice; these are of the state. Maintained by public opinion, society has common views, interests, demands. The state and society, consisting of the same individuals, interact in many and intimate ways. The state lays down the law for society, protecting and furthering society's interests; society supports the state with its economic and intellectual resources. If the society suffers, the state suffers with it, while a healthy, beneficial, and cultivated society strengthens the state and is the necessary condition of its welfare. Bluntschli further averred that German political theory, differentiating as it then did between the state and society, gave the state a firm basis and secure operation, and gave protection to society against the tyranny of the state. This is not the most extreme case of placing the state on a pedestal; on the contrary, it is a rather moderate view. However, the state is here given a life and being of its own, which is an untenable viewpoint in anthropological thinking today.

In fact, because of the views such as these, which immoderately (even in moderation) attributed an independent will to the state, A. R. Radcliffe-Brown, a twentieth-century anthropologist, rejected all reference to the will of the state, and regarded the state's power to command as a false analogy. He proposed instead the analysis of institutions of rule based on observable social phenomena: chiefs and judges are individuals in roles whereby they give commands, enforce laws, enjoy power and authority. Taken together, these roles and other like roles make up the political organization of a society. In Radcliffe-Brown's view, the political organization is part of the total social organization, and relates to the control of the use of physical force. In all societies there is territorial integrity and separateness. They engage in wars and feuds, and regulate their intergroup relationships. Each society has procedures for settling disputes and righting wrongs between individuals, and in regulating affairs touching the society as a whole. The difference between simple and complex societies, Radcliffe-Brown argued, lies in the defining and institutionalizing of these roles. Political roles in complex societies are differentiated; to the offices of king, councilor, governor, commander, are attached definite duties and privileges, defined tenure and status. Functions of law and government become institutionalized in legal and governmental administration.

Two contemporary British specialists in African ethnology have conceived the state, including the primitive state, to be an explicit form of government: Meyer Fortes and E. E. Evans-Pritchard based their views on studies of eight societies of Africa: Zulu, Ngwato, Bemba, Ankole, Kede, Logoli, Tallensi, and Nuer. The first five societies had or have a centralized authority, administrative machinery, judicial institutions, social divisions of wealth and privilege, and individual status corresponding to the distribution of power and authority

—that is, an internal hierarchical order. The last three societies are lacking in these specific forms. This second group is composed of stateless societies, each politically comprised of segments linked together, but without a higher, central office of rule. However, although lacking in specific attributes of the state, they nevertheless have some form of authority, administration, and judiciary practice. These functions are diffusely expressed in their kinship organization and in their local community life.

Is the State Found in All Societies?

The state, according to Eduard Meyer, is the unity of the political and military order of society. Without the state the legal order cannot be maintained, failing unity of will of the society. The society, conscious of the permanence of its unity, and independent of the will of individual members or component groups, is formed as a state. The state subordinates these components to its will.

Lowie has pointed out that Meyer was in reaction against an earlier idea that in primitive societies the place of the state or political order of society was taken by the kinship system or consanguineal order of society. Meyer and Lowie agreed that political order is found in the simplest societies. However, Lowie suggested an amendment: The germs of sovereignty (in other words, of the state) are found in all human societies, but at first they grow sporadically and indiscriminately; then, as the relevant institutions (associations) become more permanent and stable, the state flourishes.

Meyer developed the theory of the universality of the state in human social organization. According to this theory, human society is characterized by great variety; internal organization is complex, various parts serving various ends, subordinating one group to another in the social whole. These groups are phratries, clans, families which may spread over several tribes or sub-tribes, military and political divisions, cult societies, professional groups, village or cantonal communities.

> But among these groups, there is one which by its very conception dominates over the others: it is the one which considers all the smaller groupings as subordinate parts of a unity. It requires other groupings to submit to its dominion and constrains them to be subordinated to its will and to the ends it seeks. . . . It can itself contract by desire or by force, in a fleeting or lasting manner, with other like groups, subordinate its will to another state (e.g., as a vassal state); in contrast, it may not recognize obligations to foreign groups in case of conflict. . . . This dominating form of social group, in whose essence is comprised the consciousness of a complete, self-dependent unity, we call the State.

This quasi-poetical flight propounds Meyer's theory of the state as the organizing and governing element in any and every human group. If families are grouped into a band, then the band comprises the state-element of the society. If villages are grouped into a territorial unity, then the territorial unity, or village federation, comprises the state-element. If clans are grouped into a tribe, then that tribe is the state in and of itself. The state need have no explicit leadership by chief or king and councilors, nor separately designated judges or governmental administrators. It rests primarily on the consciousness of the group as a self-contained and distinctive unity in the conception and sentiment of the individual members. Further, it need have no territorial delimitation. The issue of the state and its relation to the social whole is clearly posed by Meyer: In every human group there are hierarchical orders, subordinate and superordinate organizational structures, and organizing principles.

Wilhelm Koppers, the late Austrian ethnologist, expressed unequivocally the doctrine of the universality of the state and its extreme antiquity. The state and society are fashioned by a human group upon a territorial base. A small band shares a bit of land, which it scours for edible plants and animals, grubs and insect larvae. Bands have autonomous control of their territory; no one else can enter and exploit it. Bands may combine under attack and form a collectivity; they are led by councils of elders and by chiefs, and they are governed by a juridical order, not by whim or force. The local band is a voluntary association voluntarily disbanded. It is more than a mere agglomeration of families, but families occupying a territory, forming a band while they are together. It is not the family but the territorial band that forms the state. The band is composed of elements found in all societies: an internal organization; a territory occupied, worked, defended; a system of custom and right making up the social order. These are social elements found in the state everywhere.

Contrary to Meyer and Koppers, we propose that human societies are of one of two kinds of political organization: (1) those with vaguely defined governmental functions which are impermanent, called into being to meet some situation as a crime or invasion, and disappearing when the crisis is past; and (2) those with well-defined, articulated governmental institutions.

Koppers argued from territory to the ideology based on territory in the band. But we have already seen that the band's territorial ideology is not that of the state. We propose, however, that, generally speaking, bands are not governed by councils of elders and chiefs with formally and permanently instituted offices. We have in mind the Eskimos, the Yahgans of the Tierra del Fuego, and the Yukagir of northeastern Siberia. At the other extreme of social organization are the complex societies organized into social classes. In these societies some people have greater power than others. But this situation is also the case among the Eskimos. It is not the power itself that is at issue; rather, it is how it is attained and retained. If it is founded on brute strength or personal prestige, these may come and go, diminished by age or slander. But if the social power is founded on a continuity of organizing principles as an institution in the hands of a few, who monopolize it by force, then we are faced with a complex society of unequals, formed into a social hierarchy which is given support by monopoly of force and expression in the state ideology. The composition of the complex societies in the formation of the state in their development is our chief problem.

L. Hobhouse, G. Wheeler, and M. Ginsberg, British social theorists, surveyed governmental functions, self-sufficiency, and internal unity of simpler peoples: Negritos of Southeast Asia, tribes of central Australia, and Bushmen of southwest Africa. Although these societies are lacking in formal offices of chief or council, governmental forms and functions are found among them, such as regulation of marriage and common defense against attack. These societies are organized in widening circles of membership: families are gathered in a broader group, as band or village, which together form the society or tribe. None of these bands is in any way a dependent body of the tribe or nation. Among yet other peoples, local groups and divisions become dependent bodies of the tribal organization, and the internal order of society thus becomes complex and hierarchical. Offices of chief and council become permanent, affirmed by explicit means—whether inheritance, self-election, or popular choice by virtue of temperament or special skill. Peoples of this sort are the Kwakiutl of northwest America, and the Philippine Igorots.

Friedrich Ratzel, a German ethnologist, had written in 1885 that even the Bushmen are not without political organization, loose as it may be, formed under a leader for chase or raid. It is by political changes in tribes that their internal organization is crystallized; and this is more than mere formal replacement of one head by another. The process is initiated by external factors of migration and conquest. States are formed out of internal self-regulation and common interest. Indefinite in extent, primitive states achieve geographic delimitation, however shortlived. Consciousness of national integration (*Zusammengehoerigkeit*) is the final state in state development. A. Vierkandt, a contemporary and colleague of Meyer in Germany, derived the concept of the state out of other materials: the inclination to social life (sociality) is a natural disposition of mankind. Social unity arose out of common activities, such as joint action against outside enemies, and shared tasks in getting a living from the environment, and by imposing a unified social force upon individuals. Society as a unity is the bearer of the moral force which is needed in defense against external attack and internal dissolutional forces. The society as such has no physical force at its disposal. The state, on the other hand, exists wherever physical force exists, in the hands of members of the society, to be used actually or as a threat against external dangers or internal disruptions. Thus, Ratzel and Vierkandt separated government of society in general from the state in particular.

Natural Law
and the Social Contract

Among those who early considered the state and society to be one and the same was the seventeenth-century British philosopher Thomas Hobbes. In his work *Leviathan*, he derived this view by identifying the establishment of human society with the formation of the state. Prior to the formation of the state, he proposed (as in the following passage from the thirteenth chapter of *Leviathan*), human beings were living in isolation from each other.

> Hereby it is manifest that during the time men live without a common power to keep them all in awe, they are in that condition which is called war; and such a war as is of every man against every man. In such condi-

tion there is no place for industry, because the fruit thereof is uncertain: and consequently no culture of the earth; no navigation nor use of the commodities that may be imported by sea; no commodious building; no instruments of moving, and removing such things as require much force; no knowledge of the face of the earth; no account of time; no arts; no letters; no society; and which is worst of all, continual fear, and danger of violent death; and the life of man, solitary, poor, nasty, brutish, and short.

The time of such conditions of life, according to Hobbes, was anterior to the formation of the state, that common power to keep all men in awe. (The state was Leviathan, "the mortal god": godlike because its awe-ful might is venerated, and mortal because it is doomed to an earthly end.) The advantages which accrue under the regime of the state are material and spiritual. When men begin cooperative undertakings, the moral order improves. Hobbes' view was that of a bargain struck: the giving-up of solitude is compensated for by gains of communal living. Men band together for their common benefit by rational and free choice, and in doing so contract to give up their freedom in exchange for life in civil society. Until that point they are subject only to the law of nature, but after making the social contract they live under the regime of the civil law. The law of civil society, according to the doctrine of natural law, is the invention of mankind, but at the same time it is derived from the law of nature. In the theory of natural law, the social order is derived from the natural order, and social right from natural right.

William Blackstone, in his eighteenth-century *Commentaries on the Laws of England,* wrote that the will of the Maker is the law of nature. Natural law implanted free will and reason in mankind as the basis for the general regulation of behavior. Human reason discovered the divinely inspired laws of nature, including the laws of human nature; our civil laws are generally based on these immutable laws and derive from them in detail. Our free will and reason make us answerable, according to our civil laws, to the divine and natural precepts governing good and evil. Thus, natural law was the raw material out of which the civilized state of mankind was wrought.

But a more modern anthropological view of human nature and of human natural law had already been formulated by another eighteenth-century thinker: Adam Ferguson wrote that art (or artifice: culture and civilization) is the nature of mankind; nature as such is foreign to the nature of humanity. If we then conclude that we grow up to be members of the human species in general by growing up into particular cultures, then we have a firm doctrine of contemporary anthropology already stated two centuries ago.

Rousseau had a different basis for the social contract than that of freely-contracting individuals. The social contract is in itself a sacred right which serves as the foundation for all other rights. And the social right is affirmed not by nature but by social convention. Rousseau's view of social right is more consistent with modern anthropological thought (although today we speak of many social orders and rights), whereas Hobbes' view is less so.

Hegel pointed out a logical fallacy in the natural-law-and-social-contract doctrine which first subjects mankind to the law of nature and later diminishes his freedom in the social contract. The state, Hegel wrote, cannot be created by law in the manner conceived by philosophers and lawyers such as Blackstone. Otherwise, the state would then stand to the superior law as a dependent body, deriving moral justification from the higher law. (Corporations stand in this way to the state.) Our view is that the moral basis for authority lies outside the state, for the state morality is part of the morality of the society in which it is found. Just as the state is a part or aspect of the political functioning of a society, so the morality of the state is a part of the morality of the society. Equality of rights and opportunities is a moral question. (It is also a legal and economic question.) The state derives or reflects the view of the society as a whole on this question, and may educate or propagandize the people about it. But if the organs of the state do not take into account the morality of the society, then this is tyranny.

The moral order of society is not imposed by the state or its dependent bodies, such as government agencies. Nor is it imposed by parts of the social and legal whole, such as corporations. The state as a part of its society shares the moral and legal order of society; if it departs radically by its actions from the dominant morality of the society, then it must use force to obtain the accord of the people. But now the force will not be imposed on lawbreakers and immoral people, but on lawful and moral people. The well-functioning state acts in conformity with the moral order which predominates in the society; the state is or should be a responsible element in society. Later we shall see how the state acts to derive its authority from the people in order to act as it does (undertakings of the early Egyptian and early Mongol states will be cited as examples).

The state, moreover, operates everywhere within the limits of society. But the corporation is not directly related to society, whether morally or legally. It is a form of association which is a dependent body of the state, mandated and chartered by the state. If the corporation acted as a state, it would enjoy political power without moral responsibility, acting at several removes from the moral order of society, and not subject to control by the latter. Irresponsible state power is tyranny.

The Corporative State

The theory of the corporative state was a device to involve the people directly in a larger whole through the fiction of unity of will, and was applied in Mussolini's Italy during the 1920's and 1930's. Adherents of the corporative state acted as though society had not articulated organs of government or divisions into stratified classes, and all were members of a great community. Ernest Barker, in the 1930's in England, was among the first to see the theoretical fallacy as well as the moral danger in the conception of such superpersonal group-persons, whereby individuality was lost in a corporate being, in the folk-mind or folk-spirit.

Again, the state has been conceived as a community arching over all communities falling within its jurisdiction. In this view, it is the dominating organ of a complex society in which many parts are fitted together, dependent on one another and acting jointly: chambers of commerce, merchant guilds, farmers' associations, labor unions, ecclesiastical bodies. Barker criticized this view for sustaining the Fascist idea of the corporative state. Just as the idea of the biological organism, with a mind and spirit of its own, is a misleading analogy when applied to the social group, and the attribution of an independent will to a social organization is nonsense, so the corporate analogy fails, and for the same reasons. The corporative state raises the idea of the corporation to a higher political and moral order than that which it corresponds to by its functions. As the overarching authority, the state is of a higher political order than the corporation-community; gliding over this differentiation is one of the moral and legal errors of the Fascist doctrine. The doctrine is not defended by making the state into a qualitatively superior political community embracing all others, for the relation of the state to the moral order of society is different from that of the communities which together form the society. The highest political order of the society is not coordinate with the entire society, with its moral, economic, and other orders. The state does not maintain a monopolistic control of the moral order of society as it does of the physical power of society. Is it conceivable that there can be two moral orders within the state?

That the state is not the sole repository of social morality is recognized in certain types of society and certain types of state. For example, in the liberal state, the society upon which the state is founded may contain more than one moral viewpoint: thus pacifists may not be shot, even in time of war, but only caused to suffer milder forms of punishment, or perhaps no punishment at all. However, there are other societies in which the state does achieve a monopolistic control over the social morality. Early states and empires emerged in which there were no discernible moral positions other than those of the states, their rulers, and the state religions. Later, of course, more articulate differences in moral tone and position appeared among groups ruled by the state as societies became more complex in structure and as individuals and classes became more conscious of their relations to the state, including the possibility or necessity of their having to have moral differences with it. Dictatorships have often sought to identify themselves with the state and in turn to identify the state with the society (the corporative state), or else by conceiving of the society as a folk or as a community, in their efforts to justify equating monopolistic control of force with monopolistic control of morality.

The issue of the moral order of the state is resolved to the detriment of individual liberty in the doctrine of the "reason of state." The pronouncement of the phrase brooks no further argument or appeal: to hear is to obey; to utter it is to require obedience under threat of the most severe penalty. Under the doctrine of the reason of state, the state is subject to no law but its own; morally and legally, the state is answerable to none. This is the doctrine of Machiavelli.

Those who adhere to the doctrine of the corporative state achieve the same end as Machiavelli, but by more roundabout means. By identifying society and the state, moral problems are not solved but created. Morals represent the views of a given people on questions of good and evil, right and wrong, and vary from culture to culture. Moral standards are relative to the culture in which they are found. In a plural and complex society, many moral views will be found, such as in the case of modern societies and the modern state. But if the state and society are identified, then the centralizing force of the state tends to make one morality predominant, and the state becomes morally sacrosanct and unassailable. The protagonists of the state may desire this end, but in a complex society, moral views in conflict with the supervening morality of the state may be found. Henry Thoreau argued against monolithic public morality in his doctrine of civil disobedience; that is, within the society, socially valid moral precepts are to be found which are opposed to the state precepts of morality. Therefore, according to Thoreau, the individual has a moral right to oppose the state on a moral issue.

Even in relatively simple societies there are complex moral structures and not monolithic ones. If one moral system is armed with the coercive power of the state, then a totalitarian morality will have been created.

Government and the State

Government in both simple and complex societies comprises formal and informal relations; the state, in complex societies, has formalized relations to a higher degree than the government of simpler societies. The formalization of a structure in the political system of a society and the formation of the state are mutually related. Ritual is a part of the set of formal relations, and the state ritual at coronations and inaugurations is designed to express the unity of the people under its central authority. But formal-ritualistic procedures and occasions are found not only among societies with the state, such as the ancient Egyptian or our own today, but also in societies without the state: indeed, the Shilluk have a ritual of the central office of kingship, although they have no state. Here, as we shall see when we examine the Shilluk case more carefully, formal ritual was separated from governmental power. Thus, government in general and the state in particular are not merely sets of formal relations. The concentration of all physical force in the hands of the central authority is the primary function of the state and is its decisive characteristic. In order to make this clear, consider what may not be done under the state form of rule: no one in the society governed by the state may take another's life, do him physical harm, touch his property, or damage his reputation, save by permission of the state. The offices of the state have powers to take life, inflict corporal punishment, seize property as fine or by expropriation, and affect the standing and reputation of a member of the society.

This is not to say that in societies without the state one may take life with impunity. But in such societies (e.g., among Bushmen, Eskimo, and the tribes of central Australia) the central authority that protects the household against wrongdoers is nonexistent, weak, or sporadic, and it was applied among the Crow and other Indians of the western Plains only as situations arose. The household or the individual is protected in societies without the state by non-explicit means, by total group participation in suppression of the wrongdoer, by temporarily or sporadically applied force that is no longer needed (and so no longer used) when the cause for its application is past. The state has means for the suppression of what the society considers to be wrongs or crimes: police, courts of law, prisons, institutions which explicitly and spe-cifically function in this area of activity. Moreover, these institutions are stable within the frame of reference of the society, and permanent.

When the state was formed in ancient Russia, the ruling prince asserted the power to impose fines and to wreak physical pain and death, but allowed no one else to act thus. He asserted once again the monopolistic nature of the state power by withholding this power from any other person or body. If harm was done by one subject to another without the prince's express permission, this was a wrong, and the wrongdoer was punished. Moreover, the prince's power could only be explicitly delegated. The class of subject thus protected was thereby carefully defined, of course; by no means were all those within his realm so protected.

No one person or group can stand in place of the state; the state's acts can only be performed directly or by express delegation. The state in delegating its power makes its delegate an agent (organ) of the state. Policemen, judges, jail guards derive their power to coerce, according to the rules of the society, directly from the central authority; so do the tax-collectors, the military, frontier guards, and the like. The authoritative function of the state rests on its command of these forces as its agents.

Theories of the State

Eduard Meyer held the state to be the political order of society, the social whole conscious of its unity. Robert Lowie, following Robert MacIver, defined the state as the political order maintained within fixed territorial limits. Paul Vinogradoff, a Russian-British jurist of the late-nineteenth and early-twentieth centuries, defined the state as a social body ("nation") orga-nized under a set of rules directing the relations and conduct of its members; as the embodiment of the power to overcome internal conflict; and as a juridical arrangement. The state as the most powerful social body and as a regulative, juridical body, must be related: regulative authority must ulti-mately have coercive force at its command.

Vierkandt admitted the state to be in only those societies which maintain physical force or the threat of its application. Malinowski similarly defined the state as the sole historical institution monopolizing coercive power con-centrated in a centralized authority. Malinowski was particularly concerned with the tribe-state, which he regarded as an executive committee of the society, with political organization, a military class, and arms as instruments of power. This phrasing derives from the Marxist definition of the state as the executive committee of the ruling class. According to Malinowski, monopoly of force gives unity to the tribe, transforming it into a state whose hegemony extends over a determined territory. Thus, the territorial delimitation of the state arises out of monopoly and unity of political power.

Fortes and Evans-Pritchard, as we have already said, define the state as a type of political system with centralized authority, administrative machinery, and judicial institutions. They say that the type of society in which the state is found has social stratification based on wealth and privilege, and differences in status corresponding to the distribution of power and authority (the greater the authority, the higher the status).

Julian Steward has analyzed three levels of social integration, which enter into the formation of the state. At the first and simplest level, societies are mere aggregations of families, or bands comprising several families. At the next higher level are groups of villages forming a society, still relatively simple in organization. The state is the highest level of integration of society, and it is in this type of society that families, village communities, and other social aggregations enter into interdependence with one another, joined into a wider and more complex unity under the state. Under these conditions, social control is brought into focus, and rules and regulations are imposed on all component parts of the society. This system of controls forms the basis of political hierarchy and a social system of classes and statuses. Governmental structure, social stratification, temples, canals, and other cultural achievements of the state appear as new institutions.

Steward's view of the various levels of integration and of the state as the overarching, highest level of integration of the various social components, or aggregates, of society was foreshadowed in a general way, but without the use of the word "state" as their term of reference, and with different levels or steps, by Hobhouse, Wheeler, and Ginsberg: (1) Self-dependent, small communities, known as *bands*, form the effective social units at the lowest economic stage, that of primitive hunters and gatherers. (2) Bands are not totally isolated, but maintain relations with similar neighboring groups with whom they share a common language, intermarry, join in religious ceremonies. Such an aggregate of bands is called a *tribe*, but has no common government or collective unity. In societies with more complex economic arrangements, tribal unity is more clearly defined. (3) Peoples with higher social and economic organization possess a common government, at the head of which is a chief or king as among Kpelle, or a council as in the League of the Iroquois. (4) Still higher in the scale are societies no longer classed as tribal. Government is now centralized, and local unities lose their autonomy and are formed into districts whose heads are centrally appointed. These are national governments, whose formative process may be exemplified by ancient Egypt, and it was referred to as such by Wheeler, Hobhouse, and Ginsberg.

Thurnwald defined the state as a political community (*politisches Gemeinwesen*) formed by the combination and stratification of peoples of different ethnic origins. In the course of their change of social form by superordination and subordination of ethnic groups, different social functions are introduced. Societies with state formation are more complex and develop later than the archaic political communities (*palaeopolitisches Gemeinde*). By referring to stratification of various ethnic groups with different functions in a single society, the *conquest theory of state formation* was reformulated.

Hegel wrote that only an aggregation of people which can combine for the common defense of the entirety of the property of its members can call itself a state. This aggregation need not be designed for self-defense but it can only call itself a state if it is *capable* of self-defense. The state is a community. Hans Kelsen, a contemporary legal philosopher, too considered the state as a community created by common legal action. Hegel's defense is one kind of common action, just as Kelsen's creation of a national legal order is another common action out of which the state as a community arises.

Such views indiscriminately involve a people or nation as a whole in common action. They do not distinguish between different social relationships to the action in question. Thus, Hegel assumed that all members defend the property of all. He considered that some have no property and are defending the property of others, but did not relate these two thoughts. Thurnwald wrote of a differentiating criterion, the various ethnic origins of conquerors and conquered, who then become related as governors and governed once the state is formed. This is in a sense an analytical approach to the problem of state-as-community, but it does not go far enough. The process of conquest by one people over another is not the sole means whereby the state is formed. And even in those cases wherein the state *is* formed by conquest, it may be that members of the conquered people enter the service of, and form part of, the ruling group.

Kelsen has raised the complex issue of the law in the state-as-community. Although the law does in fact relate all the people falling within its jurisdiction in a community of action, and the letter of the law makes no distinction between rich and poor, a rich man can more easily raise enough money to pay his bail if he is accused of committing a wrong or offense in which bailing becomes a judicial issue. A poor man cannot always do so, and may have to await trial in jail. This is contrary to the spirit of the law, since imprisonment is a form of punishment which can only be imposed if the case against the accused is adequately proved. There are many other injustices under the law, but the question of bail may suffice to make the point that the state and the law themselves distinguish between different kinds of individuals within their scope. To this extent the concept of community is weakened insofar as it is related to the state.

The state must be regarded as a more complex entity than is implied by the concept of community. Common action may make the state, as Hegel indeed has said, but may create a false sense of community, since not all men under the state stand in the same relation to the state. If we leave the field of social action and relations as formative processes of state-community, and take up community of interest, the matter of social differentiation may become clearer. The propertyless man may not have the same interest in defense of the aggregate of property in the state as do property owners.

In the writings of the Marxists, the state is more analytically treated: here there is no sense of community. (The Marxist definition of the state as the organ of the ruling class for the control of all other classes has already been mentioned.) Friedrich Engels wrote of the state as the product of economically advanced societies, in which property and privilege are unequally distributed. These are complex societies, divided into classes, of which the upper is the ruling class, superior in its social and political position by virtue of its ownership and control of the means of production—land, machines, etc. Although it does not rule directly, but through a specific social institution (the state), the ruling class maintains its position over all other classes, indirectly unifying all forms of power under its command.

The state emerged out of the process of class formation and differentiation into rich and poor, ruling and ruled. The full-fledged state, it is true, is found only in complex, class-differentiated societies; however, the formation of social classes is not the cause, and the formation of the state is not the effect, in this relationship. Rather, these processes should be viewed as interrelated: in the process of formation of classes and of class stratification into higher and lower, the state is formed; and conversely, in the process of formation of the state the social classes are formed and stratified. (At the same time, the economic product of society is unequally owned, controlled, and distributed. This will be examined in some detail in discussion of the early Slavic and Mongol states further on in this book.)

The concept of separation of state from community was developed by MacIver, who considered the state to be the organ of community, but not identical with community itself. The (political) community is made up of many associations, such as merchant guilds, churches, business corporations, trade unions, political parties, etc. Of these, as MacIver put it, the state is the most powerful, the most permanent, and the most comprehensive, being the victorious element in the social whole. As far back as the seventeenth century, Johann Althaus (or Althusius) had defined the state as the community of communities (*communitas communitatum*), one which arches over all the others under its sovereignty. While the state is a community, said he, it is of a special kind, superior to all others. Old Althaus' view is close to that of a more modern-day MacIver's.

Harold Laski, a prominent politician as well as political theorist in England from the 1920's to the 1940's, held the state to be a form of human association, a compulsory form whose compulsion over man lies in its power, from which there is no appeal. It is located in territorial society in which distinction is made between government and subjects. Laski proposed that the state is the organ of supreme coercive power, and as such it alone possesses sovereignty. The state is morally neutral, being intrinsically neither good nor evil, neither full of worth nor worthless. It is to be judged by its subjects only on utilitarian and practical grounds, by what it provides for the commonweal. It is subject to the judgment of social morality, therefore, but is not itself the source for social morality. Although, according to Laski, the supreme coercive power resides in the state, that power is in fact exercised by a government—that is, by persons acting as agencies of the state. A small number of such persons formed as a government exercises the supreme state power over the greater number of subjects or citizens of the state. Note the contrast on this point of numbers between Laski and Bluntschli, who considered the state and society to be made up of the same people.

A number of critiques have rendered untenable the idea of the state as a form of community. The Marxists attack the concept of community of interest in the state; Barker criticized the view of the state as a group-person or corporate community; MacIver made the state into the regulating organ of a politico-territorial community. (If we substitute "society" for "community," MacIver's conception accords with the view of the state advanced in this book.) Max Weber, just as MacIver and Lowie, traced the development of the modern state from foregoing associations, but unfortunately these associations cannot be defined by the ends they served, for there was no limit to these ends. According to Weber, the state can be defined only by the means which is its particular characteristic—namely, the monopoly of physical force within a territory—and thus he conceived the state to be an association compulsory within its territory.

Just as we have distinguished between stateless and state societies, so Weber distinguished between the modern and the less advancd states. The modern state, he argued, has taken over functions of institutions found in the *sib* (or clan) of stateless societies and of simple states, including the function of monopolizing all forms of violence. Weber asked how this extreme and supreme form of domination was justified, hence legitimized. The legitimation is accomplished by three factors: by the force of tradition in the hands of a patriarch; by the subjective qualities of an individual leader (*charisma*); and by the virtue inherent in rules which exact compliance simply by their existence as rules of a rational order. But Weber was speaking only of the modern state, and in so doing was overlooking the question he had raised in passing that concerned the state as a form of community.

We have mentioned Weber's idea of the formal foundation (that is, the justification and legitimation) of the modern state. He brought out as characteristic the system of order in force throughout the territory (covering both members and non-members of the state), saying that both it and the staff that administers it are subject to the effects of changes in legislation. Thus viewed, the modern state is seen to be a compulsory association with a territorial base. Movements of and within the Mongol clan, for example, are subject to approval by higher political authority, which can enforce its decisions by physical means. (The Mongol state in its flowering epoch, the thirteenth century, differed from Weber's picture of the *modern* state in its system of legislated and administered order, and in the nature of its jurisdiction: the delimitation of its territory was vague. We will see below in greater detail that territorial specificity and specificity of state functions are closely connected.) The characteristic of compulsoriness, which may be traced to the more ancient and less well-defined states, is in sharp contrast to the social life of bands whose members may opt to leave and join other bands without subjecting their decisions to approval by a central authority. The organizational feature of unrestrained mobility among bands is shared with stateless sibs and class, such as are found in segmentary societies of Africa, of which the East African Turkana are a good example.

Summary

Let us sum up the various attributes of the state manifested in the theories reviewed in this section (the parenthetical notations show to what extent the authors cited are in agreement). The state is distinct from society, and from government in general (all the authors). It is the central and highest political authority for regulation of the society (Engels, Fortes and Evans-Pritchard, Laski, Lowie, MacIver, Malinowski, Meyer, Steward, Vinogradoff, Weber). It maintains its political authority within fixed territorial limits (Laski, Lowie, MacIver, Malinowski, Weber). It is a level of integration and an instrument for integrating a number of communities and/or associations (Althaus, Hobhouse, Wheeler and Ginsberg, MacIver, Lowie, Steward, Weber). The state acts through a governmental machinery with defined agencies and divisions of functions (Fortes and Evans-Pritchard, Steward, Weber). It is formed out of a people conscious of its unity and identity as such (Hobhouse, Wheeler [although with another term than "state"], Meyer, Malinowski). The state is embedded in a type of society which is stratified by wealth, prestige, and power, and is divided thereby into classes (Engels, Fortes and Evans-Pritchard, Laski, MacIver, Steward). The state is maintained for such common action as defense and internal regulation (Hegel, Kelsen). The source for moral judgment of the state lies outside the state (Engels, Hegel, Laski)—contrary to Machiavelli, who taught that the state is answerable to no other body than itself.

Malinowski held that in the state, monopoly of coercive power and the delimitation of territory are connected. This interconnection is an integral part of the state, being in and of its nature. Or it may be understood historically, as a sequence of events, whereby power was asserted in a geographically unified and defined society. When a central authority establishes a monopoly of coercive force in a society, the limits of extension of that force, which may have been vague until then, at this point become precisely determined. Those over whom the force or threat of force is exercised must accept the state or reject it. There is no middle ground.

The state is an organ of complex society. A society may be complex in the sense that it is composed of a number of sub-unities, such as villages, guilds, parishes, unions, corporations, and brotherhoods, existing side-by-side. All these are kinds of associations (MacIver, Lowie, Weber). Alternatively, a complex society may be composed of upper and lower ethnic groups, classes, castes, or social estates. Usually, association and stratification go together. The state is conceived to be an institution which arches over the coexisting smaller unities (Althaus, MacIver, Steward). It is formed in stratified societies; state power is in the hands of the higher social stratum. The hierarchical order of society in which the state is formed, the hierarchical order of the state organization, and the role of the state in maintaining the hierarchical order of society, all are interrelated.

Consciousness of membership in a society is heightened as the society is demarcated by territorial limits and inner structure. Conscious membership in society and in a social stratum is further developed by the formation of the state. These social conditions help in the process of state formation. A stratified, centralized, and precisely delimited society, conscious of itself, makes a social cause and issue of its being. These are ideological commitments, such as nationalism, the veneration of the state as such, etc. The presence of these ideological factors is also a sign of the formation of a complex society; these factors, to the degree that they are consciously developed, are measures of the degree of development of the state.

The state is the ultimate organ of power in any society in which it is found. It is an organ for social integration, internal regulation, and external defense. Societies lacking the state accomplish these same ends by other means, but the state performs these services *for* society, and in so doing also serves its own ends. Although integration, regulation, and defense are primary functions of all social groups, the state combines these functions with the promotion and preservation of its own existence as an end in itself. Thus, the state is to be viewed as a *secondary formation* for the achievement of the aforementioned social ends. It is *among* the formal organizations which function in this way, but it is the *sole* formal organization which combines all these functions. The state also is a secondary formation in that its self-perpetuating, self-serving "political" incorporation comes demonstrably later in time than does its organization as a structure designed to serve society. As we have said, and as we shall see in the case of Egypt and Mongolia, the state serves to integrate society, but under its own sovereignty.

The state preserves individual and collective rights of property, privacy, and survival, maintaining the social order *per se:* an attack on an individual right is also an attack on the social order and on the power of the state to maintain it. The state defends from attack the territory which it rules, not only because the territory is useful for the maintenance of its subjects, but also because loss of territory is at the same time a diminution of state power. Therefore, the veneration of the state, the cult of the state, and nationalism all are developed as ideological expressions which serve the ends of the state rather than the ends of the society. It should be pointed out that because these ideological expressions at the same time serve the ends of the social class which is most closely associated with the state, the state is "secondary" in yet another way—as a secondary organ of social integration, because it serves the needs of the different social classes unequally.

Two *Government*
without the State

There are many kinds of government. Complex societies, which usually have explicit and formal sets of rules to govern their social classes or castes, have similarly complex, clearly demarcated, and formal governmental structures forming their organization framework as states. At the other end of the scale are the simple governmental practices and institutions of the hunting bands— Eskimos and Australian aborigines, for example. However, no matter how simple, none of these peoples is without a form of government. In between are societies that lack the state, but nevertheless having state-like governmental institutions, whose social and governmental order is more complex than that of bands.

Institutions of government which are state-like in form and function, but which are not themselves states, exist in societies having somewhat more advanced governmental institutions than the Eskimo. These are more or less formally constituted institutions such as secret religious societies, military and police associations, high councils, divine kingship, or the dependency of a particular clientage to a political superior. One effect of such institutions is to counteract and overcome the individual's bonds of local kinship and community: unless there is a means to reach out beyond the family or band into which one is born, the extent of polity and political action is limited. Activities such as membership in secret associations and political councils, and personal allegiance to chief or king, involve the individual in affairs which extend to the limits of the tribe, to the entire people. The relationships of local life are thus enmeshed in the larger whole; wider outlet is provided for tensions and conflicts generated within the small group; greater choice and freedom of outlook and action are created; social lines may be drawn among many villages, parts of villages, and families joined in common cause. At the same time, relations to secret society, council, chief, or king place new constraints on the individual and on the society.

Peoples with state-like institutions are often lacking in some vital particular which might contribute to the formation of the state among them. The Plains Indians had well-developed associations of adult males which were autonomous or quasi-autonomous, with police and military functions. They also had a high office of chief, and often a council of the tribe. However, as Lowie indicated, the power inherent in the offices of chief and council was weak, and the offices themselves were often ephemeral. The general pattern of Plains tribal social control was simple and informal, working against the concentration of power in a center of authority, and the associations acted together to prevent any single association from becoming the dominant force in society. Thus in maintaining, together with chief and council, political order within the territory of the tribe, associations were state-like in *function*, though far from state-like in *form*.

A number of West African peoples, among them the Kpelle, had a formally constituted office of king, or high chief, which potentially might have provided the nucleus for a centralized and formalized state power. However, at the same time the Kpelle also had secret religious societies, which performed some of the functions of fully developed states. The power in Kpelle was therefore dual, resting in both king and head of secret society; each prevented the other from achieving the ultimate degree of political control.

Government by chief and by council or some other kind of corporative association, then, are alternative to rulership by the state. Although all of these differ from the state in the low degree of centralized political power and of permanent, specialized organs, they are nevertheless all explicit modes of government. There are still other forms of government, on the other hand, which are not explicit, and are even simpler. These last will now be examined in reference to Eskimo, Australian, and Andamanese societies.

Simple Government in Bands

Eskimos

The Eskimos, who live in Alaska in bands of usually no more than 50, are sustained by fishing, by hunting whales, seals, and other large sea mammals of the Arctic, and by tracking down or trapping land animals. They have neither chiefs nor advisory councils, nor deliberative assemblies—although they do practice a form of individual economic leadership: in whale-hunting, the boat owner has dominance over the crew, and primary right over the catch. Nevertheless, they have no formal government and no explicit organs whereby they are ruled; they are without specialized administrators, judges, courts, and written law. Rather, they have informal means of controlling aggression among people, and righting wrongs. Their primitive legal mechanisms include (for example) the song-duel. Someone who has been physically injured or defamed, or has had property stolen, makes an accusation in public. Plaintiff and accused become challenger and challenged, meet before the assembled band, and compete in alternate singing. The injured recounts the wrongs done to him and seeks redress; the defendant asserts his innocence and otherwise defends himself. The decision between the accuser and accused is made by the community.

The Eskimos countenance several socially acceptable modes of doing away with people: suicide, senilicide (killing of the old), infanticide, and invalidicide. Homicide is sometimes redressed by blood revenge. A single murder, as E. A. Hoebel has put it, is avenged by the kinsmen. The public or society at large is not involved; it is a private wrong. (In contrast, murder is considered to be a public matter in more advanced societies, and the individual cannot seek private redress. The entire society, through the state organs, necessarily interests itself in murders in the American and in similar societies.) However, *repeated* murder among the Eskimos is in fact considered to be a matter of public interest; it is a public crime of which the band must take cognizance, and is punishable by death at the hands of a chosen agent of the band. The Eskimos have a simple form of governmental regulation of social behavior: their court is not a permanent institution; it is convened as the occasion warrants, and after the judgment the court is disbanded without fixing a time for reassemblage.

Australian Aborigines

The Dieris of central Australia and their neighbors also live in bands. Their government is somewhat more formal than that of the Eskimos; that is, Dieri governmental functions and roles, and qualifications for filling them, are more explicitly recognized by the society. The old men rule, in a form of government known as *gerontocracy*. Among the tribes of Northern Queensland all the old men rule together, and at no time do they appoint a chief. On the other hand, the Dieri are governed by a council of old men; one of these is chosen as chief, and rules while the council is not in session. Within the Dieri council, decisions are taken unanimously. These Australians are all simple peoples who live by hunting animals of their vicinity and and gathering wild plants, and insects and their larvae. Hobhouse, Wheeler, and Ginsberg have noted that no more than 50 people live in any local group, and that of these the elders are five or ten in number. (Eskimo bands are of approximately the same size.)

Andaman Islanders

Radcliffe-Brown made a study of the Andaman Islanders, who are Negritos (pygmies, black-skinned) living on two islands in the Bay of Bengal: on Great Andaman where they live in ten tribes, and on Little Andaman, in three. Each tribe has distinctive dialectal and cultural characteristics which mark it off from its fellows. These tribes are not political units, for they have no significant functions of this nature; each tribe is composed of about ten subordinate groups, and these form the political-governmental units. Each such group is autonomous, and is usually composed of some ten families, or 40 to 50 people who jointly control an area of about 16 square miles, which is their commonly recognized hunting territory. Andamanese governmental administration is not the task of a separate and specialized set of people, but is placed in the hands of senior men and women acting together within each group. They make decisions, providing the group with advice and counsel. Leadership is based on prestige, for which personal characteristics in an Andamanese are sought: seniority, skill in hunting or war, liberality, and an even temper. Men with these traits rank as leaders; their opinions carry weight, and they are voluntarily supported by their juniors, a factor which engenders informal relation of leadership and following. Authority is exerted by virtue of a personality type; it is not formally established, maintained, or handed on.

To repeat: the societies we have been considering illustrate governmental practice of a low-keyed, informal kind.

Associations and the State

Societies are formed on the basis of principles of kinship and territorial neighborhood. Members associate within societies for specific purposes: to preserve the civil order; to express common interests or achieve common goals; to establish or maintain religious cults and orders. Membership in associations is based neither on kinship nor on common residence—members may live here and there in the society, or even internationally. MacIver defined associations as organizations in a society composed of members joined for a common end, and the state as the most permanent and comprehensive of associations. The state, according to MacIver, is an authoritative association, exclusive in membership in the sense that one can be an active citizen of no more than one state; it is a central institution of government whose purpose is to maintain and develop the rights and obligations of a community. Lowie called attention to the state-building potency of these associations, since they break through the kinship and neighborhood organization of society. Fulfilling functions of their own, such as religious or police service, they tend to relate people on broad territorial lines. Moreover, associations have rules of membership in keeping with their purposes: e.g., adult males in a society joined in the veneration of a deity, which is their common purpose in coming together.

Associations build states by breaking up traditional bonds and local forms. Broad and precise territorial delimitation provides for the establishment of the political order of the state, a condition beyond the reach of illiterate, simpler peoples. But are associations enough? Crow associations could put their own welfare before that of the social whole. This particularistic tendency was overcome only by submitting all the Crow to a single authority (although such control was achieved only intermittently): out of economic necessity, in the hunt they temporarily suspended that freedom from coercion by social authority which the tribesmen usually enjoyed, and which was reinstated afterwards. The Crow had not achieved a state form by the time of U. S. conquest because they did not render permanent the superimposed coercive authority. Herein, according to Lowie, lay the tendency toward the formation of the state, but not the achievement of the state itself.

The hunting and police associations of the Plains were attempts to establish monopolies of physical force in a society. But they were unsuccessful attempts: each police association was limited in power, hemmed in by rival associations. Nevertheless, Lowie regarded them as first steps in state-formation, since Crow society at large recognized (at least on the occasion of the buffalo hunt) that one or another of these associations, through its members, had the moral and legal right to lay violent hands on any member of the hunt who had been adjudged guilty of an infraction of a rule of the hunt. The society at large delegated authority to act in this capacity on such occasions, and recognized the police association as the delegated acting authority. The Plains association in this limited way established, or at least contributed to the establishment of, a central authority which on occasion monopolized the legal application of physical force, or the threat of its application, in one institution.

Ernest Barker further developed the relation between the association and the state, arguing that society grew around the state, and cited the example of the formation of a nascent society around the Virginia and Massachusetts Companies (later, states of the United States of America). The state thus was the core around which American society grew, the legal organization of the new society: the state was the skeleton, society the soft parts of the being. Now these companies, just as the British or Dutch East and West India Companies, were originally commercial ventures sponsored, advanced, and protected by their home governments. During the sixteenth, seventeenth, and eighteenth centuries, many associations for profitable exploitation of new continents were formed. However, the mandates which they received in London or The Hague were so vague, the bonds of communication with the mother countries so loose, that the companies were able to establish firm hegemonies in many parts of the world. Moreover, their political-commercial ventures were favored by the absence of firm polities or military opposition in the territories they discovered and conquered. Thus, the Massachusetts and Virginia Companies were able to act as though they were states, and eventually to form nuclei out of which states emerged. An association budding forth from an older state, developing political strength and advancing to a state form of its own, the United States at the same time contributed to a new society, the American.

Associations did not build a state in the New World out of nothing, nor is there evidence that associations have so acted anywhere else. The materials were provided by the social origins of the colonists who came from European societies which were organized as states. Barker added materially to Lowie's conception: without a doubt, association contributes to the process of state formation. It is equally clear that association is not the full or sole basis of state formation.

Plains Indian societies had explicit associations with political functions:

maintenance of order throughout the tribe; limitation and restriction of local loyalties; tying the community to the larger whole.

Indians of the Plains:
Crow Government by Associations

Lowie has described the governmental arrangements of the Hidatsa, Crow, Mandan, Blackfoot, Dakota, and Pawnee—all hunting peoples who lived in villages, whose total population was 10,000 at most. The office of head chief was an established institution among them but was not hereditary; to it was allocated only a modicum of political power. The tribal council, composed of elders and outstanding warriors, had limited authority among these peoples. The head chief was the first among equals: here Lowie applied the old formula of feudal England, whose king was then the first among his peers, the barons—*primus inter pares.* The Hidatsa chief received credit when buffalo they hunted were in good supply, or if his people were victorious over their enemies. He was held accountable if the hunt was poor or the battle lost.

The work of government of the Plains Indians was done by a number of clubs, or associations, whose relationships Lowie likened to chapters of a European religious order. The Plains associations had social, military, political, and ceremonial functions. The Crow had eight such associations, to which any adult male Crow was freely admitted on application.

Crow politico-military associations bore the names of Foxes, Lumpwoods, Dogs, Bulls. Members were added by annual election; leadership was in the hands of nonelective elders. The associations had four explicitly recognized functions:

1. Military defense of the entire Crow society in case of war.
2. Direction of the communal buffalo hunt (the chief of all the Crow appointed one of the associations to police the hunt each year).
3. Social-ceremonial rehearsal of dances.
4. Mutual help for all members of the club in the purchase of the "sacred bundle of the individual."

In directing the buffalo hunt the association in charge had the power to administer corporal punishment and confiscate the kill of any hunter who started too soon or took more than his share. In case of extreme offenses the association could destroy all the property of the guilty and even put him to death. The buffalo hunt police role ended with the hunt, to be reactivated the following year, possibly by another of the hunt organizations (Foxes one year, Lumpwoods the next, etc.). Buffalo-hunt police could not act outside their sphere of activity, which was the regulation of the hunt and punishment of those guilty of disobeying the hunting regulations. In the event of a homicide which was not a direct infraction of hunting procedure, buffalo police pacified the victim's kin, but did not themselves punish the offender.

Plains associations were corporations—that is, mutually independent associations in perpetuity. Each maintained an internal unity, even though it was inactive much of the time. All were part of the larger social whole. They were rivalrous, even antagonistic toward each other, often disrupting the civil peace, except when all the associations were subjected to the control of a single authority during the hunt. The effect of these associations was to reinforce territorial definition and unification, as part of military defense and hunting regulation. They loosened neighborhood and consanguineal ties, strengthening feelings of tribal unity and giving guidance in crisis to the social whole.

In addition to these police-*cum*-military associations of the Plains Indians there were religious cult organizations, such as the Tobacco association of the Crow and the Dakota dream cult. Again, craft specialists—tanners and porcupine-quill embroiderers of the Cheyenne and Western Dakotas, for example—formed associations of their own. The effect of these associations on the society as a whole was to reinforce the police and war associations.

The office of chief on the Plains was limited and ill-defined; it was a social role in the acting-out of which the principal took no initiative but carried out decisions of the council. Nor was the tribal council effective in unifying and integrating tribal societies on the Plains, being neither a permanent nor regularly constituted institution. Plains society in general, as their institutions of government show, failed to establish a stable order of sociopolitical and territorial integration.

The Sacred Kingship of Shilluk

Leslie White has pointed out that in early states, such as those found in ancient Egypt, Mesopotamia, and China, the religious and secular orders were one, forming the state-church or church-state as an integrating and controlling mechanism of society. J. G. Frazer, in his work *The Golden Bough*, also wrote of varieties of sacred kingships in the ancient world. He cited as an unusual case the peculiar Roman arrangement of the purely symbolic, ceremonial king, without power of authority over people, "reigning," as it were, side-by-side, with the emperor of Rome, who wielded great power, both political and religious.

Aidan Southall has referred to certain traditional African kingdoms as "segmentary"—by which is meant a whole composed of parts that are readily joined or separated, without a developed degree of mutual interdependence. Moreover, in any segmentary polity, the local chiefs or other authorities do not give up their power to the central ruler; the political power remains in their hands. Nevertheless, a central office may be established in these kingdoms with a symbolic function of representing the unity of the people and the land.

In any state the people, through their local leaders acting as their representatives, delegate authority to a central office. Thus, a two-way stream is created: delegation of authority and obedience to authority. But the segmentary polity, according to Southall, is lacking in regular, stable, popular recognition of a central office with coercive power. These polities are not ruled by administrative organs of society composed of integrated parts. Indeed, life goes on in the village, the villagers often unaware of events in the capital or royal court. Wars and dynasties come and go, but the villagers pursue their own affairs: raising cattle, planting, marketing, tending to their families. The kingdom of Shilluk is such a segmentary polity.

Dinka and Shilluk peoples of the Sudan live along the Nile Valley and speak Hamitic tongues akin to ancient Egyptian. They have been described in the older ethnographic accounts as having in their polities the office of king. As did other peoples we shall discuss, they maintained that there was a close connection between the special powers and physical condition of the king and the condition of the soil (he was also the rainmaker), and the cattle. Thus the king had to be vigorous in order to ensure the health and prosperity of the people. If he showed evidence of physical decline, the Dinka considered that he had outlived his usefulness, and killed him. If he contracted bronchitis, he was laid in the midst of dried and burnt cattle dung, and his people danced around his resting place, raising dust so that he either was asphyxiated, or coughed himself to death. The dead king-rainmaker was then buried in the cattle byre. (The Dinka believed that he took the food of the community into the grave with him so that next year there could be food.)

Evans-Pritchard has critically evaluated the ritual murder of the divine king among the neighboring Shilluk, and concluded that there is far more at issue. The Shilluk today number about 200,000; their habitat is the treeless savannah of the Sudan. They live by agriculture, supplemented by a modest amount of cattle-raising. In the recent past, their hamlets were made up of from one to 50 households, each hamlet comprising an extended family or a grouping of extended families in a small lineage; lineages were grouped into clans. The hamlet chief was the chief of the lineage of which it was composed, if a lineage was found in only one hamlet; alternatively, the hamlet chief other than the lineage chief was subordinate to the latter if the lineage comprised more than one hamlet. All the lineage chiefs were in form but not in fact subordinate to the king, *reth*.

In each settlement there was a dominant lineage and a dominant hamlet; immigrants and strangers in the settlement formed a separate community with its own corporate lineage. The settlement chiefs were chosen from the dominant lineage, supported by the strangers and newcomers, and were confirmed in office as a matter of form by the king of Shilluk. Some of the stronger lineages were branches of the royal clan; these were more powerful than the resident dominant lineages, and could choose the chief of the entire settlement. In general, however, settlement unity and chiefly authority were founded on integration around the dominant lineage. The chiefs represented their people in inter-settlement and inter-clan affairs, and hamlets were gathered into districts for common defense under their chiefs.

Members of lineages and the parent clans were descended from common ancestors. Lineages were formed by branching off and colonizing a new territory. Both clan and lineage were exogamous, and even when dispersed, members of different lineages within a clan did not marry each other. The wife commonly came to join her husband, but if a man resided in his wife's lineage, their offspring belonged to her lineage. Thus, lines were grafted onto each other.

Since all Shilluk were joined in a common polity, the Shilluk kingdom was composed of segmental settlements existing side by side. The degree of control and direction from the central authority was formal and minor: settlements conducted their own affairs, and sometimes combined in ephemeral groupings with neighboring settlements. The Shilluk land was divided in two parts, northern and southern, the royal settlement occupying the center. Settlement chiefs as a rule had no hereditary status, there being two exceptions to this: Ger of the northern Shilluk, and Luak of the southern.

The office of king was the single functional as well as geographic center of the nation. Kingship was hereditary, and in the twentieth century was traced back to the founder over 31 generations. Only the son of a king could be raised to office; male descendants of dispersed branches of the royal clan were ineligible. A pregnant wife of the king returned to her natal settlement to bear the royal offspring, and the son of the king was raised by the chief of the settlement, the mother's brother. The king's daughter was forbidden to marry, thus avoiding possible conflict over the succession; the king's son on marriage established a hamlet near that of the mother's brother. Some of the king's sons were downgraded—declared ineligible for the kingship—and could then intermarry with the parent clan.

The Tonga settlement of Shilluk played the leading part in the royal funerary and investitive rituals. Tonga daughters were always among the king's wives, who smothered him to death under circumstances which will be described shortly.

Shilluk aristocracy was formed of descendants of past retainers of the kings. These comprised dependents who placed themselves under royal clientage; certain homicides; persons possessed by the spirit of the first king, Nyikang; poor men who attached themselves to the court. There was a loose social hierarchy in the royal house: the royal family; nobility composed of other members of the royal clan; and commoners, including persons originally clients—supporters and dependents of the king.

Although the king was both the secular and the spiritual head of Shilluk, his power was limited. He did not nominate, and had no veto power over the election of, clan chiefs and chiefs of settlements or lineages, but merely confirmed them in office. The king had only sacerdotal status; he reigned but did not rule. He functioned as high priest, presiding over the rain sacrifice and rites at military victories. The spirit of Nyikang participated in the supreme deity, Juok, and in the reigning king. Divinity lay not in the person of the king but in the office of kingship; the distinction between the two was clearly made by Shilluk. Thus, Shilluk rebelled on occasion against individual kings while preserving the office of the kingship intact. Their ideology included the possibility of rebellion against the reigning king in the event of national disaster—a plague, a defeat in war.

Shilluk moreover differentiated royal clan from nation, as they did king from the kingly office. Regicide touched the person of the king, not the office, and the royal clan, not the nation. Regicide, therefore, was not a ceremonial act on the national scale; its political scope was as limited as the political power of the king. Although he united the nation symbolically, and his dissolution was connected with the dissolution of the Shilluk as an entity, his symbolic value was, as we have seen, divested of real power over people, except as it applied to his position as chief of the royal clan. The identification in spirit of the physical well-being of king and kingdom derived from the mystical value of Shilluk kingship. If the king was weak the kingdom was weak; if the king was senile the kingdom would fall into decay. Therefore the king was killed before he grew old or sick, in time to save the kingdom. (Evans-Pritchard maintains that the practice of regicide did not touch the divinity of the office.)

The activities of the royal office were severely constrained, and because of this, inherent tensions around the office gave rise to the fiction of a national act of ceremonial regicide. But ceremonial regicide was not an affair of the nation. Election of a new king, on the other hand, *was* a national affair, in which all Shilluk chiefs participated, and all the Shilluk people through their chiefs.

The king was surrounded by his court: retainers, clients, kin. He had no governmental machinery nor administrative structure beyond the royal court, and they had no delegative powers. Therefore, in the absence of the qualities of administrative authority and appointive or delegative powers, and despite a kingly office and the mystique associated with it, the term "state" does not fit the Shilluk case. And failure of the Shilluk to extend the powers inherent in their kingship to the actualities of temporal rule was not the only barrier to their development of the state; the economic basis was lacking as well. Although the kingship symbolized the unity of the Shilluk, the symbolic unity was of little further consequence in national economic relations and political action. In short, the Shilluk have a highly developed identity and consciousness as a people, but they have a kingdom without a state.

West Africa

Kpelle Secret Societies

The Kpelle of Liberia and neighboring Guinea are a people who live, by gardening, in permanently settled villages. Their population has numbered about 400,000 in recent years. Traditionally, the Kpelle were divided into royalty, nobility, free commoners, dependents, and slaves; the freemen held themselves to be the original settlers of the country.

In order to understand the political and legal system, a word about the kinship pattern is necessary. Kpelle traced descent from father to son, but children were raised by the mother's brother—that is, in the mother's *patriline*. The mother's brother could place the child in pawn to relieve himself of an obligation, and the child's father could not protest this act. However, property passed from father to son, following the descent line. Father and son felt close to each other, and could not be required to bear witness against each other.

The society was divided into groups of patrilineal descent, each ruled by a chief. Over the whole people was the king. The chief of a patrilineage could place his kinsman, even if he were a freeman, in pawn against an obligation incurred; the mother's brother could place his sister's son. But freemen could not otherwise be bought or sold. Slaves were primarily war captives who had not been ransomed; to a lesser extent slaves were made by debt or crime. Slaves could buy their freedom, and freemen could pay their own way out of pawn. Children of freemen were free, whether the mother was a free woman, dependent, or slave; children of female war captives were free; children of unmarried slave women were slaves.

Dependents were children of slaves and their descendants, and those who entered into dependency by their own act (through poverty or need for protection), or who were given by their parents as gifts to the king or to a rich and influential personage. Their descendants could not be sold or given away. A form of dependent was the client who entered into a personal attachment to a master, or who agreed to serve the master in return for maintenance and protection. They had their own garden plots, and could not be sold into slavery or given away. Clients of the king and of the lineage chiefs even enjoyed influential roles at court.

Kpelle had developed a system of secret religious societies, six in number, of unequal prestige and power. The greatest was the Poro. A seventh society reached beyond Kpelle. Membership in a secret society was limited to one sex, and membership was a prerequisite for marriage, public office, and participation in rituals, including one's own burial. It was difficult indeed for the uninitiated to establish residence or otherwise enter into normal Kpelle life. Even strangers sought admission into the secret societies to obtain or enhance their social status. Kpelle youths entered the secret societies at puberty or adolescence to assure a respected place for themselves.

The Poro society dominated the secular and religious life of the Kpelle; it was the basis for secret society activity, as well as for regular tribal activity. The head of the Poro society was elected in secret conclave by prominent Poro members; he was considered to be immortal and his death was kept secret. He was held to be invisible to those outside the Poro society, and enjoyed a supernatural mystique. Novices entered a probationary period before their election was confirmed in the Poro society. They were reborn on initiation, their debts were canceled, and they broke with their own past. Within the Poro society there was a special bond among those who were initiated at the same time. Initiation included indoctrination into the secrets of the society, which were religious by nature, and training in male Kpelle virtues of obedience and fortitude. Novices were given athletic instruction, and taught to hunt, fish, weave, and work iron.

Prominent Poro members could gain admittance into more secret organizations, with further mysteries and greater mystique attached to their membership. Within the secret-society system as a whole, magicians received training in their special arts, commoners received training in the arts of everyday life, and sons of noblemen and chiefs received training which would be useful to them: court ceremonials, rules of successions, access to special tribal traditions relevant to their rank, and the essentials of indigenous polity. Thus the Poro and related secret societies were operational elements in the social and political organization of the Kpelle.

While the Poro society was the male tribal association from which children, the women, and aliens were excluded, the Kpelle women had their own secret society, the Sande, a counterpart of the Poro. Girls joined the Sande at puberty and were trained for three years in household tasks, dancing, and sex hygiene. The head woman of the Sande was supposedly endowed with power to bring fertility to mankind.

Other associations—namely, the Snake, Antelope Horn, and Gbo—had restricted rules of membership and geographic distribution. The Snake secret society possessed a monopoly of magical treatment of snakebites; its headmen were descended from a serpent and were without fear of snakes. The Antelope Horn society was an association of magicians who determined which sorcerer and which form of sorcery was the cause of a death; they also exorcised demons. Closely related to the Poro, they were the religious police of the tribe, and were outside royal control. The Gbo was also closely related to the Poro; the headman of the Gbo could transform himself into the chief of the Poro. Payment of an initiation fee was necessary for admittance into the Gbo, whose initiates had powerful antidotes against death by sorcery and poison, and could eat bewitched rice.

The Leopard association extended beyond Kpelle and was widespread in Liberia and neighboring Guinea and Sierra Leone; its cult was the veneration of a fetish. The form of worship included human sacrifice to avert evil for the entire tribe. The executioner was a member of the Leopard society who would put on a leopard skin, and in the course of the sacrifice cause the victim's blood to fall onto the fetish. The body of the sacrifice was then cut up, the flesh eaten, and the hair and nails set aside for magical purposes. The Leopard association sometimes acted as the agent of the Poro association, and thus gained a temporary dominance in Kpelle life, and in the lives of neighboring peoples, as far as the Ivory Coast and Portuguese Guinea.

Another type of association of the Kpelle was the men's house, a place where men of the community could gather, and from which women, children, and strangers were excluded. Here the men gossiped, dried fish, plaited mats, bartered, argued suits of law. Corpses lay in state before the men's house, prior to burial. The social functions of the men's houses paralleled those of the secret societies, although membership in the men's houses was not formalized. Here, too, opinion was formed, and bonds were established between men not otherwise related: channels for relationship and communication aside from the bond of kinship were thereby opened up, and alternative bases for common action established.

Kings and Clients

The Kpelle king was the supreme ruler in name; the highest court of appeal in law, ultimately deciding all questions of civil peace; the owner of the soil; the controller of men's fates. In actuality, the power of the king depended on his personality rather than on his royal status. Above all, however, the king depended on prominent members of the Poro for support in all great questions. The chief of the Poro convened influential members of the secret society, who were at the same time influential among the entire Kpelle people; he was the alternate pole or center of political authority. Within the secret society the chief could impose penalties, including the death sentence.

The Poro did not possess the highest political power, but neither did the king: there was a balance of forces between the two, and decisive power shifted from one to the other. This is not a case of rebellious authority which either overcomes the kingship or is suppressed once for all; the alternative centers remain stable, polarized against each other.

In *theory*, the king was privy to all Poro affairs, and was sometimes referred to as its real head; in *fact*, the Poro chief was a countervailing political power, independent of the king. During the four-year probationary period of the king, the head of the Poro assumed political dominance in Kpelle. He summoned the council of the entire people, and regulated internal affairs and international relations. During his tenure, external war and internal litigation were equally prohibited. That the head of the Poro could neither conduct war nor hear disputes was a profound constraint on the power of this office.

Just as there was a disharmony between the office of head of the Poro and that of king of Kpelle, there was a disharmony between the Leopard association and the general Kpelle society. The Leopard association at times achieved a dominant position in Kpelle affairs by taking chiefs and powerful persons unto itself. Whenever the Leopard association became too powerful, violent public reaction arose against it, and the people required the chiefs and king to punish membership in the Leopard secret society with death.

In general, West African kingdoms in their traditional forms, including Kpelle, failed to centralize political power in an office, whether that of king or head of a secret society. Centralization was rarely realized in full, and was hemmed in by opposing centers of power. These polities included personal bonds of master and client, and councils of leading tribesmen-subjects which, acting either formally or informally, provided a further limitation on concentration of political power in one office.

Relations among the different Kpelle social strata were not severe and distant, and the power of the king was relatively weak; the secret societies overcame the bonds of local territorial and consanguineal allegiance, and undergirded the identity of the whole Kpelle polity no less than did the king-subject relationship. The king was in *theory* the ruler of all Kpelle, including the Poro society under his power; *in fact* there was overlapping of personnel, in the complex of client relationships. Nevertheless, the offices of king and court stood at the head of a set of local ties and arrangements, and stood *for* them, and as such were in opposition to the principles represented by the secret societies.

These contradictory tendencies were not overcome in Kpelle social and political organization. These people have long led a settled life, with a simple form of agriculture and marketing of products; they had a national political system and conducted international relations of their own, not only between kingdoms, but also in the Leopard association. Their social and political organizations had wide areas of latitude for the amassing of local power and followings by political leaders. But internal organization of government was simple rather than complex; missing are the permanent, articulated, specialized institutions and organs of government for which we have been probing. The Crow and the Shilluk developed institutions having a *potentiality* for forming a state. The Crow police association overcame local ties of kinship and community; the Shilluk sacred kingship constituted a symbolic center of the entire people. But the lack of a permanent and powerful center of the Crow polity and the lack of power of the Shilluk royalty negated their respective state-forming processes.

The MacIver-Lowie approach to state-formation via associations is valid, but is to be supplemented. The Crow police association and the Shilluk kingship are important for another reason: as specializations of function. For it is by further development of specializations of social functions, and their sharp delimitation, that the state is formed. The kingship and the police are but two such specializations. The Kpelle difficulty was that whereas the principle of (secret) association acted in one way to overcome local bonds in support of the over-all political unity of the society, the principles of kingship and of the master-client relation acted in another. The first principle, shared with the Crow association, was canceled by the second, shared with the Shilluk. For these reasons Crow, Shilluk, and Kpelle cannot be said to have realized the potentialities of state formation. Now what can be said of them in this regard is that they developed certain institutions which we account relevant and useful in state formation.

There are various reasons behind this limited political development. The possibility of a state is out of the question in the case of the Crow, for demographic as well as economic reasons. There is no absolute population figure below which it is impossible to form a state. However, even relatively simple and traditional states have populations hundreds of times greater than the Crow. The Crow economic functions were unspecialized: every adult male Crow did more or less what every other adult male Crow did to gain a living for his family. Again, Shilluk and Kpelle polities had populations a hundredfold, and twice that, greater than that of the Crow. But population size is not a sufficient condition for the formation of a state, even though it is a necessary one (states, after all, have been formed in societies with populations of the same size as Kpelle). Finally, the existence of central institutions such as those of Shilluk and Kpelle are necessary but not sufficient conditions for state formation, just as was the police-military association of the Crow.

With this survey of positive and negative factors in state formation, of why some societies made progress toward the state without going the whole way, we bring to a close the discussion of societies without the state.

Three Ankole:
Formation by Conquest

The state traditionally has been developed in societies with large populations (numbering at least in the hundreds of thousands) whose institutions of political and military power have been directed by a central authority which has (at least symbolically) represented the society as a whole. Since state functions are continuous and durable, state institutions must be manned by people who are not primarily engaged in economic production, but are free to concern themselves with affairs of state. This condition had already been achieved to some extent by the Shilluk and Kpelle, although economic specialization was not achieved by these peoples to the degree found even in simple traditional states. Nor were related economic conditions achieved by them: the formation of the social whole with integrated economic and political parts, social stratification, and specialized agencies of political authority.

We will now turn to Ankole, a traditional state in the socially stratified society of east Africa. Ankole met, in a limited and qualified way, the conditions we have discussed—which causes us to qualify it as an *emergent state*, and no more. But a state of sorts it was, headed by a king who was served by his ministers, his court, and his clients; a king who ruled by virtue of the

43

power of his office over the social classes, each class having different economic and political functions.

The Conquest Theory
of State Formation

Ratzel conceived of state formation as being the result of the external processes of migration and conquest. I.. Gumplowicz and F. Oppenheimer further developed the conquest theory of the state. Their researches have been surpassed in part, but are of continuing interest because of the discussion which they provoked. Gumplowicz held that warlike hordes migrated into the neighborhood of peaceful cultivators and husbandmen and forced them to give up a part of their products. Out of the meeting of two heterogeneous peoples, one peaceable and the other bellicose, the relation of ruler and ruled was established, the relation which is the mark of every state community (*staatliche Gemeinschaft*).

Oppenheimer was more sophisticated: to him, the state is a social institution forced by a victorious group upon a defeated group in order to regulate the dominion of the victors over the vanquished, securing itself against revolts from within and attacks from without. The primitive state was the creation of warlike robbery. The state in general is an organization of one class dominating other classes, this class organization being the result of conquest and subjection of one ethnic group by another. In support of this thesis, Oppenheimer cited Wilhelm Wundt, a German psychologist, and Ratzel, who in turn mentioned the Arab conquests of the Near East and North Africa in the seventh century, the Mongol conquests of Asia and Europe under Chingis Khan, the Magyar conquest of Hungary. The materials which Gumplowicz and Oppenheimer knew best were of the old Austrian empire with its many peoples—Austrians, Hungarians, Czechs, Slovaks, Slovenes, Croats, Italians—all with their aspirations and struggles for freedom. The conflict and subordination of nationalities in that empire down to the First World War provided materials for the conquest theory by these writers.

Oppenheimer has been identified with the Marxist doctrine of the state; but he rejected this idea. Engels had defined the state as the organ of the ruling class for the domination of all other classes in society. The state, according to Engels, is not one with society, but is a part of it—a small but all-powerful part, developed only in complex, stratified societies. But it is not ordinarily founded solely by conquest of one ethnic group, tribe, or nation by another. It may be, but more significantly the forces of development of the state are internal to the society: a people increases its sources of wealth by advanced economic organization, technology, and control of natural resources. The economic goods produced are unequally distributed, and one class of the entire society controls a greater amount than any other. More importantly, the ruling class has a greater share of the land, cattle, and other means of economic production, and by using its greater part in the economy, it is able to assert control over all the other social classes, which are now inferior to it. The means whereby this control is achieved is political force, including physical power. The highest (that is, most centralized), tightest, and most monopolistic control of the political power resides in the state, which is the organ of the ruling class. Marx wrote that the history of society is the history of class struggle which is created by inequities in the distribution of social wealth and power.

The conquest theory engendered considerable further discussion. Richard Thurnwald related material from east Africa to the conquest theory of the state. And there is no doubt that conquest played a part in most if not all processes of state formation. But only a part. Lowie and W. MacLeod noted that Oppenheimer wrote not on the origin of the state, but on the origin of social stratification. M. H. Fried has developed this thought further: the type of society leading to a state formation by conquest is a superstratified society, given that the victors, or both conquerors and vanquished, have been internally stratified already.

The conquest theory failed as a general theory of the origin of the state because it introduced only external factors, and failed to take into account internal processes in the formation of a given state. Migration of a bellicose people to the vicinity of a peaceable one or the converse, and subsequent conquest by the former of the latter, does not in itself lead to class stratification and state formation. There must also have been beforehand at least the germ of social stratification, of an administrative system, of an ideology of superiority and of rulership, and of a burgeoning economy with some differentiations of economic functions. The Eskimo and neighboring Chukchi, for instance, made war upon each other, with occasional conquests, but we do not speak of a Chukchi or Eskimo state.

Ankole: Background

The discussion of the conquest theory of the state has indicated that in the process of state formation, external factors of invasion and forceful subjection of a weaker people by a stronger are less important than internal development factors. Nevertheless, in certain cases states *have* been formed by conquest, and among these can be listed Ankole in east Africa, which has been well described by K. Oberg, an American ethnographer. The Rift Valley of east Africa is long and narrow, with a dense agricultural settlement. This narrow, grassy belt, favorable for stock-breeding and agriculture, brought farmers and herdsmen into close contact. Oberg has hypothesized that this contact, and the ensuing conquest and reduction of farming Bairu to tributaries, provided the basis for the formation of the Ankole kingdom.

Ankole was a small native kingdom of western Uganda, near Lake Victoria, with a population of half a million. The kingdom was formed of an earlier-settled, Bantu-speaking, agricultural people, and a later intrusive, Hamitic-speaking, cattle-raising people from the north. The cattle-raisers first settled among the Bantu, then conquered and ruled over them. These pastoral people call themselves *Bahima* and called the agricultural people *Bairu*. The Ankole kingdom was one of a series of political formations by pastoral peoples who migrated from the north and settled among agricultural peoples along the Rift Valley from the Upper Nile to the mainland part of Tanganyika (present-day Tanzania). At first the Bahima and Bairu lived side-by-side but apart; then, after conquest, the Bairu provided food and labor for the conquerors, economic exploitation and political domination proceeding hand-in-hand. Out of this set of relations the Ankole state was formed.

According to Bahima tradition, these pastoralists were once united in the Kitara empire, which was then dismembered, its components forming the ruling strata of the old native kingdoms of Nyoro, Toro, Ankole, Ruanda, and Buganda. In the process of conquest, most of the descendants of the Kitara empire identified with the polities which they came to master; the Buganda rulers alone continued to regard themselves as intrusive.

Also according to Bahima tradition, a mythical folk called the *Chwezi* appeared from the north and consolidated the Kitara kingdom. Strong and handsome, great warriors and powerful magicians, but few in number, they lived by pastoralism and hunting, on milk, meat, and honey-beer. Their great leader Ndahura had magical powers and brought fertility to the people and the land during his brief reign. But misfortune followed, the cattle died, and all the Chwezi fled but one, Ruhinda, who returned to found the dynasty of Ankole. The Bahima believe that the Abachwezi are not dead, but will return to rule in Ankole; they venerate them in sacred places. The cult (which is not adopted by the Bairu) is closely related to the system of rule.

The Bahima believe that prior to their conquest of the Bairu they had no kings, but followed rich and important men who led the people and settled their disputes. They did not war against the Bairu but peacefully exchanged pastoral products of milk and butter for agricultural products of beer and millet. The Bahima proved that they were superior in war, applying techniques of herd domination to human domination. They now live in large, fenced settlements—*kraals*. Their settlements are larger and better defended than those of the Bairu, who live in extended families in small, separate homesteads. Bahima were traditionally organized in clans ruled by chiefs, and in smaller groups of unilineal descent, forming units of political and military cooperative enterprise. Internal cooperation against external aggression was highly developed.

A caste division existed between Bahima and Bairu, respectively superior and inferior in legal and social status. The Bairu were in turn divided into serfs and slaves. Bahima and Bairu did not engage in joint military actions; Bairu as lower caste were prohibited from military service. Still, crossing of caste boundaries did take place: the Bahima took Bairu concubines; and in fact if the Bahima father had no other children, those gotten by the lower-caste concubines became his heirs. Children of unions between Bahima chiefs and Bairu concubines formed a separate sub-clan, the half-caste *Abambari*.

The Office of the King

Ankole was ruled by the Bahima king, to whom the lesser Bahima stood in relation as clients. Clients took an oath of allegiance, and paid a royal tax in cattle and in service. They followed the king in raid and war, receiving in exchange for military service cattle taken as booty. Individual relations between king and client could be denounced by either side: the disruption of the relation of clientage became an act of rebellion when undertaken by a group of clients, but then, too, if the king did not share out booty taken in a raid, his client-following might accuse him collectively of betrayal, and seek his overthrow.

Great natural and supernatural powers were attributed to the king. He bore the appellatives and honorifics of Lion (fiercest of the cattle raiders), Bull (which causes the cattle to multiply), Land of Ankole (which he swallowed whole), Drum (which maintains the unity of Ankole), and Moon (which drives away evil and assures good fortune). The king had to be virile, and was administered a fatal poison prepared by magicians if sickness or senility overtook him.

In the king's hands lay the highest administrative power, against which there was no appeal. He alone had the right to send off a raiding party, make war, declare peace. The king had appointive powers over the posts of military leaders; drumkeeper, who was always chosen from a particular clan, but had to be acceptable to the king; personal servants, who were always drawn from particular clans, but again had to be acceptable to the king; favorite chief, or *Enganzi*. Royal appointive power was not nominal but included the right of veto, in contrast to that of the Shilluk king, whose power was confirmative and nominal.

On his accession to the kingship, the king (with the advice and consent of his mother and sister) chose the Enganzi from among the chiefs. The Enganzi had to be from another clan than the royal clan, and could not himself become king. But he was king-maker, prime minister, and war minister. He proposed names of military leaders to the king, serving together with the royal mother and sister as a chief royal adviser. Below them in access to the king and the ultimate authority stood the executive chiefs—leaders in war and collectors of tribute. The royal kraal was made up of a large following of magicians, servants, wives, and guards. Craftsmen working in iron, leather, and wood, and the king's personal water carriers, wood-choppers, and butchers, formed a personal following to the leader. Also supporting him was the royal drum cult, symbolizing the unity of Ankole under him, the royal status in Ankole, and the royal power over Ankole.

Royal tribute was collected from Bairu serfs by district chiefs of the Bahima, who retained part of the levy and transmitted part to the king. Also, direct tribute, collected and forwarded by the Bairu, was imposed on the Bairu by the king.

The king was the highest judicial authority under Ankole law. He had the power to sentence to death, to exile, to torture and curse, and to confiscate property of those who broke the law. However, in Ankole there were sanctuaries which, if the accused and the guilty could reach them, placed them outside the royal power.

Succession passed from father to son in the royal line, the right to succession normally being weighted in favor of the eldest son because he usually was the strongest: the successor had to be strong enough to fight off his fraternal rivals. Sometimes the successor was not the eldest son, but the strongest and therefore most favored; sometimes the succession fell to the son endowed with the most powerful magicians and retinue (often including his mother and sister, whose magic was not derived from the royal line, but was their own). Unsuccessful rival siblings were killed or exiled by the victor.

During the war of succession, which might last several months, the realm was in chaos. The royal place was filled by a mock king who was without power—perhaps a common Bahima herdsman—who was killed on the accession of the new king. The old Enganzi, as his last act, enthroned the new king, who then (following the advice of his mother and sister) appointed a new Enganzi. During the war of succession, the great chiefs stood guard in the border areas; being without right to the succession, they were disinterested in the struggle. The struggle for the kingship was a test of physical and magical powers, of ability to lead, kill, influence: a test of the courage and the social and supernatural powers of the future king. The successful candidate necessarily had to have the highest powers to assure good fortune during his rule.

Social and Political Organization

Traditional Ankole society was stratified into higher and lower castes, which were further divided into social estates: nobility, commoners, serfs, and slaves. Stable and institutionalized sources of power were developed around the king: favorite chief, border chiefs, royal mother and sister, magicians. The king ruled through his personal following. These corporate bodies undergirded the kingship; they did not normally seek to diminish and destroy it. The border chiefs preserved the territorial integrity of Ankole and extended its influence and power by raid, conquest, and defense. Ministers, magicians, and royal kin lent their support to the kingship, if only because their powers were linked with the kingly office and were dependent on the kingship.

The following features of Ankole polity are offered as a minimum set of political conditions of the *emergent state:* territorial integrity; unified political organization of the people; concentration of power in the hands of the central authority; actual unity of sacred and temporal powers of the kingship; partial but actual and not merely nominal delegation of power by the central authority to ministers, local leaders, cult leaders, and magicians. Acts of delegation of authority were circumscribed by rules; powers delegated were circumscribed in their sphere of activity. These delegated powers were at the same time institutionalized; the incumbents might be liquidated, but the offices were not.

The unity of the polity of Ankole was symbolized in the office of the king and the royal line of descent, in the myth of origin of the polity, and in the honorifics and titles of the king. By way of comparison we may note that kings of ancient Egypt and Mesopotamia had qualities and titles other than those of the kings of Ankole. They defined their polities in different ways, and delegated powers to different offices. However, the articulation of separate and specialized functions, partial delegation of state temporal and divine power to ministers, and institutionalization and stabilization of these offices, are to be noted in all these early states.

Thurnwald's Theory

This description of Ankole substantially corroborates Thurnwald's hypothetical view of the formation of states by conquest in east Africa; he advanced the following argument. Population density, measured by the number of inhabitants per square kilometer or square mile, is much lower among pastoral than among agricultural peoples. Through migration, the population density of pastoralists becomes even thinner. Heads of families become more independent during migration than during stable periods, and the traditional clan forms tend to break up. During the process of migration and decomposition of the pastoral clans, prominent personalities are able to come forth who otherwise would have been constrained by traditional social structure.

According to Thurnwald, agricultural communities lived side-by-side with sedentary communities of artisans-craftsmen, and with primitive food-gathering tribes before the formation of the state. Exchange relations among the three economically specialized components—farmers, craftsmen, and gatherers—were maintained; their relations were as equals, without higher and lower social estates. Social life was organized in segmented, independent communities, each with a collective economic life.

Pastoral peoples migrated into the area of the already existing complex, at first dwelling peaceably in its midst. Then by military action, the segmentary, intertribal relations as among equals ceased. Farming, artisan, and gathering peoples were now stratified into higher and lower estates dominated by the pastoralists, who provided political focus. New, independent pastoral clans ruled over clusters of erstwhile cell-communities of the other three specialized ethnic and economic groups.

During the migration and residence in the neighborhood of the sedentary peoples, pastoralists developed a spirit of personal enterprise and they learned to "herd" peoples as they herded livestock. The pastoral estate first lived in independent unities, but later competed for extended control over each other and the newly dependent social units. Cattle herds became symbols of power as well as actual wealth. Various powerful families formed noble houses and dynasties, the formation of the noble stratum being developed by *primogeniture*—seniority of the line descended from the firstborn son. Following their conquest, the pastoralists increased their private family property in herds; agricultural families accumulated private property in land. Noble houses of pastoral conquerors acquired house slaves, who formed a separate estate; tribes of craftsmen, dependent on the pastoralists, formed a separate caste. War captives and strangers formed lower social orders but, unlike the castes of craftsmen, could rise in social estate.

Thurnwald took the religious organization as further evidence of the relation between the older kin-based communities and the later state structure. Secret religious societies were of two types: societies in conjunction with a state formation bore an aristocratic character; in contrast, non-aristocratic, secret societies, such as the Poro of the Kpelle, arose in societies without a state. Lowie has indicated another difference: membership in secret societies developed in a state context required a high initiation payment; the basic Poro initiation was not so, although entry into other Kpelle secret societies did require heavy payment. Secret religious societies in east Africa, as opposed to west African Kpelle, were open to all castes and both sexes, and thus formed an egalitarian counterpoise to the highly stratified lay society.

An assessment of Thurnwald's picture reveals that at one time indigenous tribes of cultivators, craftsmen, and food-gatherers lived side-by-side in east Africa and the Sudan, and that later, pastoralists migrated into the Rift Valley, subsequently conquering the local peoples and forming the Buganda, Ankole, and other kingdoms. The formation of class and caste strata with the pastoralists at the head of the political hierarchy followed the conquests, but may have already begun during an interim period of peaceful coexistence. Thurnwald criticized Gumplowicz and Oppenheimer for having derived class stratification exclusively out of the frictional belligerency of the pastoral conquests; the process was overemphasized in their conquest theory. He held, nevertheless, that conquest theory was applicable to Ankole where social stratification, the domination of the many by the few, and domination of conquered people by the pastoralists, contributed to the formation of the state.

Thurnwald's conception provides insight into the process of state formation in east Africa, including Ankole. However, we should know more about the Chwezi (Abachwezi) and Kitara political enterprises, whose ideology, as seen from the tales and myths of Ankole and neighboring peoples, may now be reconstructed and analyzed. Moreover, the various forms of the tales and their political burden should be compared. Thurnwald's argument that the conquering pastoral peoples learned the "herding" of men from their herding of the livestock may be translated as an extension of the concept of the ecological dominance of man over the herd to the political domination of man over man. The difficulty here is that Thurnwald read too much into the ecological as the basis for the political relation.

The Emergence of the State

As we have seen, the limitations placed on Kpelle political development were overcome, for there was no opposing pole of power to the kinship. The different functions of society in Ankole were increasingly developed by the introduction of a central authority; the different social groups and communities were consequently better integrated into a larger whole. But the integration was still incomplete and defective, and the low degree of community integration was paralleled by the low degree of integration of state power. The border chiefs were powerful inhibitors of kingly power, and different parts of the kingdom, communities under border chieftainships, continued to live separate lives. The peoples performed the same tasks and were dependent on each other for exchange, but only to the limited degree mentioned. Hence the kingship and the state acted as a crowning, necessary integrative force, but there was little to integrate and little integration to represent, by comparison with modern states. There must be clear differentiation, separation, and mutual dependence before there is integration.

Authority of the state issuing from above and obedience from below requires the participation and agreement of the people, which was not the case in Kpelle, but was developed to a limited degree in Ankole. The measure of that degree may be ascertained: the conquest state was ruled firmly by the pastoral Bahima. Master-client relations extended and deepened the power of the monarchy over the entire polity. But the agricultural Bairu were not greatly touched by the sovereign power; living in their separate villages, the Bairu kept their own speech. Ankole was not an integrated state with one language. The Bantu farmers were kept out of the royal affairs, and royal cult wars of the pastoralists, yet they were brought into public affairs as taxpayers.

The degree of complexity in organization of the economy and society of Ankole corresponds to the degree of complexity of their polity: government was characterized by a high degree of formalization, and a modest degree of specialization of function. The central and highest office was the kingship, expressed in the greatest ceremonial formality. The cult of kingship had a symbolic value signifying the unity of the people under the kingship, in the Bahima conception. Thus cult, office, and ceremonial meaning were unified at the highest level. Yet while the royal power was monopolistic and without rival, the capacity to delegate it was relatively weak. The economic communities were poorly integrated into the political whole. These were the limitations on the Ankole polity. Nevertheless, we propose that Ankole constituted a state within its own society. Domination of man by man, concentration of authority backed by force, and threat of force and supernatural power, were all well developed. The king ruled both symbolically and actually. Perhaps we can see this point better by contrasting the Ankole case with others—with Shilluk and Kpelle.

Neither the Shilluk king nor the Kpelle king had complete monopoly of power to rule. The Shilluk king was a symbolic ruler; local chiefs had powers which did not derive from the king and which lay outside the kingship. The Kpelle king was constrained from monopoly of power by the office of head of the secret society. Kingship and statehood, however, are different; Kpelle and Shilluk kingship were not embedded in a state polity. In Ankole, on the other hand, central authority was well established—power was largely focussed in the hands of the central authority and then delegated (it was, however, limited by the presence of lesser but independent chiefs). In sum, Ankole was a simple, traditional, even primitive state, based on conquest.

Four Egypt: Formation
by Internal Development

At the beginning of the twentieth century, ambitious writers claimed for Egypt the honor of having been *the* source and fountainhead of all civilization—of writing, of great architecture in cities, of the formation of the state. Today we would smile at enthusiasms on behalf of such a dubious cause, knowing that but *one* of the earliest states which can positively be identified as such was formed in Egypt. Other state formations were created in Egypt's time—some linked through diffusion, some independently developed by parallel processes. On the basis of Egypt's case alone, it is not hard to see that too much has often been made of the race for the chronological championship.

Egypt was in cultural contact with Mesopotamia as well as with other parts of the Near East in prehistoric times, taking the lead in certain developments while being follower and recipient in others. Thus, during the fourth millennium B.C., there were several centers of culture and politics in Egypt which were in contact with Mesopotamia and with each other, exchanging goods and techniques, combining with each other to war on other peoples, and fighting among themselves. The various political centers of ancient Egypt were first unified under two realms during the fourth millennium B.C., and then joined into one during the period of unification, 3400–3200 B.C. In the following century Egypt established its first historical dynasty. The state did not come into being precisely at the moment when Upper and Lower Egypt were unified, however, nor was the state founded by the founder of the first historical dynasty. The state had been formed *before* the unification; state-forming processes and unifying processes in the society mutually supported and consolidated one another.

The record of state formation in ancient Egypt is somewhat fuller than that of state formation in Ankole. Evidence of formation of the Ankole state was derived from comparatively meager sources: from the inner dynamics of contemporary political organization, from their folk traditions, and by comparing them with their neighbors. In addition to these techniques in the study of the beginnings of the state in ancient Egypt we are aided also by archaeological and historical records introduced shortly after unification of the kingdom. Through pictographic and other cultural accounts, our knowledge of Egypt in the early period of its history as a state is fuller than is that of many another nascent state, even from later times.

Social Life

The cities, towns, and villages that constitute the locus of Egyptian civilization are contained in a long and narrow tube following the valley of the Nile, constrained from spreading far from that abundant source of water by great deserts to east and west. The Nile rises far to the south of Egypt and is seasonally fed by monsoons, which annually flood its banks, providing water which is conducted to the farmlands by artificial irrigation channels. The record of the Nile extends over a period of many thousands of years, and the river is not once reported to have failed in its annual flood. The northernmost limit of Egypt is the delta of the Nile, which empties into the Mediterranean.

Archaeological evidence from the burial sites of Neolithic farmers of Egypt contains no indication of differences in social strata; all people proceeded to the afterlife as equals. Moreover, the cultural differentiation between Upper and Lower Egypt was not clear-cut; the culture of the Nile delta and valley was spread throughout the area and was at that time archaeologically homogeneous. Evidence of class divisions, of centralization of rule, and of geographic-political delimitation is missing in the early millennia of agricultural Egypt; the demarcation of political areas and areas of different material cultural remains is to be noted only as the unified state came closer to its ultimate realization at the end of the fourth millennium. A realm was then formed in the region of the delta, which is Lower Egypt, and a second in Upper Egypt, to the south. The first ruling dynasty of all Egypt, in combining the two geographic regions, formed a political and cultural whole. At approximately this time, written history in Egypt began.

Tombs of the late predynastic period (fourth millennium B.C.), shortly before the imperial unification, reveal increasing differentiation between rich and poor. Villages of this period were distinct from urban centers, with which they were in economic interchange. The towns were ceremonial as well as mercantile and political centers, each with its surrounding cluster of villages. The population raised a primitive form of wheat on lands irrigated by channels along the Nile Valley, and domesticated sheep, goats, asses, and ducks. In this epoch, according to Eduard Meyer, were the beginnings of the Egyptian state; the system of states of Egypt was already in being at the time that Egyptian history began.

Egypt had already developed a system of irrigated agriculture at the beginning of the historical period, and evolved a stratified social order with division of labor into peasantry, craft specialists, supervisory personnel, and so on. Examination of the skeletons of the period of the two kingdoms indicates that the inhabitants of both kingdoms were people of the same physique. Pottery and field and household implements from both sites point to a common cultural continuity from an archaic period when techniques of material culture were more primitive and social organization was simpler. The political system of these kingdoms of Upper and Lower Egypt was evolved by indigenous processes, and was probably not founded upon foreign invasion and conquest.

To judge by the excavated skeletons, at the time of unification, people with a different physique appeared who may have come over the sea from Mesopotamia. They were bigger-boned than the native Egyptians, resembling Mesopotamians of that time. Also, stone carvings in Egypt depict a landing and conquest by a folk who sailed in high-prowed ships of a type found in Mesopotamia. The trends toward class division and political unification that were already present in Egypt at the time of its conquest by these invaders were gradually intensified and accelerated. At the same time, a common language emerged: there is no suggestion that Egypt had large unassimilated speech communities within its homeland during the imperial period.

During the Neolithic period of prehistoric farming, social and political organization was simple. Villages were strung out along the Nile, there were no great towns or ceremonial centers to insinuate their many cultural and political influences, and cultural life was homogeneous. Political unities were organized on a small scale; tribes or clans were headed by chiefs. Social life of the period was divided into mutually similar compartments; villages and village clusters were self-sustaining and independent.

From Clan to Empire

Social organization during the transition from the local village to the centralized empire became increasingly complex. As villages joined together in ever-larger polities, social distance between upper and lower classes was extended and deepened. Territorial bounds and bonds were established, lines of demarcation between political divisions were drawn, and segmented organization ceased to be. The Egyptian term for these political divisions was *spat*, which, according to Alexandre Moret, formerly designated a kinship unit, and later an administrative unit. Moret had written that, in prehistoric Egypt, villages and village clusters were identified by their respective emblems or fetishes. A tradition set down in the sixth dynasty, mid-third millennium

B.C., refers to rulers of these earlier village clusters, recalling a time when men were ruled by *Saru*—possibly elders of the village (or clan). Kings arose alongside or over these *Saru* in the predynastic period.

The *spat* was transformed from an economically and politically independent unity to a dependency of a politically centralized power. Meyer, followed by Moret, traced this development under the phrase, "from tribe (or clan) to empire." The *spat* ceased to be an independent tribe (village cluster, clan) and became a province of the empire; its chief became a district governor.

The districts were the cells out of which the larger polities arose, eventually combining into the Egyptian state. In the process of state formation, tribes defeated and absorbed other tribes, and, similarly, tribal gods absorbed other tribal gods and their sanctuaries. The internal composition of society was transformed from a set of homogeneous, segmented parts to a more highly integrated system composed of specialized, articulated, mutually interdependent parts. These latter parts were divided into higher and lower castes (or classes), each caste (or class) in turn divided into professions: the lower orders were divided into cultivators, potters, smiths, carpenters, and the like; the higher into priests, noblemen, chiefs, ministers, and royalty.

Egyptian land and polity was not called Egypt by the Egyptians; that term came down to us from the Latinized Greek word *Aigyptos*. The land that the Egyptians farmed in the Nile Valley they called *kemt*, "the black land"; the surrounding desert *teshret*, "the red country"; and they referred to their own land as "*to*." Egypt was called *Mizr* by the Semitic neighbors; the Egyptians referred to themselves as "the inhabitants," *rome*. Even this, however, was not their ethnic name. In fact, the Egyptians lacked the unifying symbol of a name; their unity was symbolized in the kingship and its emblems.

Ordinary people of Egypt down to the fourth dynasty identified themselves by their mother's descent line, even though wives joined their husbands upon marriage. After the fourth dynasty, children were identified by descent in the father's line. Women had a certain amount of freedom of choice in marriage, and could repudiate their marriage partners on payment of an indemnity; and wives' property rights were equal to their husbands. (But inheritance of property in historical times passed from father to son.)

Normally, in spite of the fact that all were subject to the king's law, Egyptian life was smooth and orderly. Although he possessed supreme authority, and enjoyed many royal prerogatives, the king himself could not rule by whim or fancy, but was subject to customary duties and obligations. In these favorable circumstances, social mobility was such that persons of lowly origin, even captives in war, could rise to high places.

The pyramids symbolized the magnitude of pharaonic power. Their remarkably skillful construction, vast size, and sumptuous furnishings required the mobilization of a huge portion of the resources—mental, physical, and monetary—of the country. According to official doctrine, Egypt owed everything to the king-god Menes, who by means of supernatural power had redirected the course of the Nile. Therefore the passage of succeeding kings (heirs to his powers, which were vital to the survival of the country and colored the meaning of life therein) to their afterlife required the total spiritual and physical involvement of the country. The burial pomp of the nobility was in accordance with their relative social position; the common folk were buried simply.

The First Kings of Unified Egypt

The Greeks and Romans were taught by learned men of Egypt that the first king, Menes by name, unified the two kingdoms of Upper and Lower Egypt, and established his capital at Memphis, toward the end of the fourth millennium B.C. The record of his reign had been preserved over three millennia by Egyptian priests.

Archaeological excavation has unearthed a curved slate depicting events of the life of another early king, identified as Narmer. The carving of Narmer has a number of scenes showing the figure of the king to be larger than it would have been had it been drawn to scale. His greater stature is determined by his greater status; Frankfort refers to this as *hierarchical scaling*, the application of social values to those artistic. The scene in the slate carving is a battle; King Narmer is larger than his own followers and of course much larger than his enemies whom he has defeated, including their leader. By way of contrast, a battle scene carved on a knife predating the slate of Narmer shows no hierarchical scaling.

However, Narmer had no great funerary monument erected in his honor, and this is taken as an indication that he was not the first king of unified Egypt. It is now considered that Hor-Aha was his son, the first king of Upper and Lower Egypt, the same person as Menes, to whom a great tomb and shrine was erected. But these are symbolic relationships: if Hor-Aha, or Menes, was the son of Narmer, this is to be understood in its mythical and ritual sense, and not literally.

Under the rule of King Menes, the upper and lower realms of Egypt were unified. He was believed to be divine in his person, so great in power that he was represented to be superior in physical attributes to all other men. The new king had been based in the south, and his unification was actually a victory of the south over the north; however, the dynastic concept signified unity of rule over all parts of Egypt, and not the supremacy of one part over the other. Symbolically, Memphis, his capital, was established at the apex of the delta, the point of juncture of the two former realms. Thenceforth the single realm was ruled by monarchs who, it was thought, combined the attributes of earthly and divine rule while the enemies of Egypt were a conglomerate of many powers, lacking an outstanding head. Egypt was the superior power by virtue of having this kind of king, supernatural and actual; the enemy was lesser by this standard.

During the period of consolidation of rule over Egypt, great technological advances were made: large-scale use of metal in the fields, in the town crafts, at the court, and in the army. The pictographs had been until then non-standardized representations which are interpreted only with difficulty by modern scholars. These representations were now standardized into a form of writing, the Egyptian *hieroglyphics*. Specialists in record-keeping applied the hieroglyphics in their craft, and increasingly, these and other specialties were functionally demarcated from each other. Egypt had advanced from a simple to a high culture, now intensifying further development in the same direction. Social stratification was firmly implanted in the Egyptian society and polity. Society was divided into higher and lower classes; the realm was centralized and geographically delimited.

Spiritual and secular power were joined in the royal office at the end of the fourth millennium. The king was a god-king, combining the order of the natural and supernatural worlds. At birth he was Horus, the hawk-sky-god, and representation of the royal power; at death he became the god Osiris, whose cult J. G. Frazer, in his famous *The Golden Bough*, related to the farming cycle of burial (planting) of the seed and its rebirth as grain. The cycle of birth and rebirth and the agricultural cycle of seed and grain were repeated in the cycle of the annual Nile flood and in the cosmic cycle of the heavens. The kingship was the point of juncture of the natural and divine orders: the good of the people, the state, the world of nature and of supernature, were united in the royal office. As Horus, the king brought discord to an end, pacified antagonists within his realm, and incarnated in his person the coalescence of sacred and secular rule on earth.

In contrast, the Mesopotamian kings were not considered divine; they were priest-kings whose duties were threefold: to interpret the will of their god, to represent their people before the god, and to administer by divine mandate the realm of the god on earth. The Mesopotamian priest-king was divinely elected but was not himself divine. Therefore, he could be substituted for to protect the royal person when the realm was faced with disaster. The substitute not only stood in place of the priest-king, but was the means to learn the will of the god. It may have been that the king had served the god so poorly that the disaster or misfortune was his fate, and his continuation in office imperiled the welfare of the state. On the other hand, it was conceivable that the gods intended to protect their chosen instrument. Therefore a royal substitute was chosen to learn the will of the god. In the absence of proof that the god had recalled his mandate to the priest-king, the people would not call for his replacement.

In Egypt there could be no substitute for the king, since the king was the god in his earthly manifestation. If his effectiveness was impaired by physical disability or mental decline in senility, he was put to death. But no Egyptian could take the pharaoh's place, or put another in his place: the act would have been sacrilege.

The Egyptian doctrine of the state related the king to the social whole. The state was in the service of the pharaoh; his people did not labor for the commonweal, but for the honor and glory of the king. He was the owner of all the land and of all that grew on it. Thus, Egypt was not a commonwealth, but a royal domain. So ran the theory of A. Erman and H. Ranke, two German Egyptologists. In fact, however, people lived their own lives, some even acting in defiance of the official doctrine.

The earliest kings of Egypt united in their office the sole source of authority, having been confirmed in this role by the people. They divided the authority into parts, delegating their powers through various offices:

Vizier—steward of the entire realm, royal councilor, transmitter of the royal decrees

Treasurer of the God-King—gathered the royal levies, arranged mining expeditions, controlled foreign trade

High Priest—supervised the ceremonies of royalty and also, as architect, supervised all the king's building programs

War Leader—conducted military expeditions

Agricultural Minister—in charge of the fields, and master of the livestock

The delegation of royal power evolved only gradually. For example, even down to the fourth dynasty (about 2800 b.c.), the office of vizier was not fully separated from that of the kingship, since it was traditionally delegated to a prince of the royal house. Delegation of power proceeded regionally through appointment of local governors and town mayors; regional authorities were military as well as civil officers. Ultimate coercive force rested in the hands of the god-king, who retained power to appoint and dismiss, and to impose his commands. He was the source of justice and law, and maintained control over written records.

At the royal center, government offices were not rigidly separated in function, and although new offices were introduced from time to time, flexibility of operations was maintained. In the fourth dynasty one Methen, a kinsman of the king, was Scribe of the Exchequer, Physician, Judge, and Supervisor of the Flax. He had been a district leader early in his career, then governor of three provinces in succession. At that time, too, a special chief was appointed to command fortifications against invasion by desert tribes, and to campaign against Libyans to the west, Bedouins in Sinai to the east, and Nubians to the south.

Over the course of early Egyptian history there was a struggle between the royal power at the center and the power of provincial leaders. At first the king had unified the realm, combining the various territories under their chiefs, whom he made into local administrators. Thereby, hereditary offices and properties were not separated from the authority of the kingship. However, after the establishment of dynastic rule, private property in land became more strongly developed, passing from father to son; indeed, landowners in the provinces during the sixth dynasty turned their estates into manors, and the great landowners ruled these lesser courts. But in the twelfth dynasty central power was restored when the king, who had lost control over the land, regained it.

The second divisive element in Egypt evolved in the persons of the officers of regional rule, the governors of provinces. At first these officers were under strict control of the royal house. But then the governors' powers developed; they ceased to rule by authority of royal appointment, and their offices became hereditary. Finally, after a thousand years of dynastic power in Egypt, the governors succeeded the landed gentry as the major threat to the central power. But this threat, too, was inexorably overcome, giving way to a new centralized power, after the twelfth dynasty.

Egyptian life was formed around the village, where economic goods were raised and exchanged. Here the chief had his residence, here disputes were heard. Ancient Egyptian village clusters (which became the district, or *spat*, of the dynastic period) formed groups venerating the same supernatural being, an emblem with its own identity, name, and visible representation in stone or pottery. These representations as pictographic forms were continuously maintained from predynastic to dynastic times; in the dynastic period, the representations evolved into legible hieroglyphs which are interpreted today as hawk, jackal, gazelle, lapwing, terebinth, mountain, scepter, sistrum, bull, and others. Whether the villages and village clusters had names is not known to us; their objects of veneration are. One of these emblems, the hawk, became the symbol of the monarch, a god who in his earthly manifestation was the king.

It is not the people who were divided into social groups, but land which was cut up into districts corresponding to the aggregations which constituted the state, over which the state ruled as the highest integrating institution. Whenever the state grew weak in its central rule, the districts accordingly increased in power; their leaders actually strengthened their hands at the expense of the royal right. Pictographic representations of the hawk, jackal, and other emblems were carried into battle as ensigns.

The Narmer slate and other palettes and plaques of this time pictographically record the series of political and military events—mainly battle victories—by which the tribes of Egypt confederated first into two kingdoms, then into one. In these battle scenes it is an emblem or a leader identified thereby which acts in battle, destroying the enemy fort or trampling the enemy troops. The falcon or hawk, the fish, the scorpion were incarnate in the divine being of the king, and incorporated in his quality and title. The king was the falcon, Hor(-us), and bore that name in his title; he was the fish, Nar(-mer). Thus, Narmer may not have been the personal name of the king, and the attribution may not have signified a particular person, just as the title Horus designated not one king but the line of kings, the royal office. For this reason it is possible, as we have suggested above, to think that the succession from Narmer to Horus (or Menes) was not an actual but a symbolic event.

Moreover, the ensigns which accumulated about the royal office may have had several meanings. They may have referred to lands and peoples brought under the power of the victor in battle. But some of the manifestations of the pharaoh had a functional significance, regardless of territorial or ethnic origin. Thus, the king as the god Horus represented the political-integrating function of the pharaonic power. The king as Scorpion had an economic function: pharaoh as the force of irrigation of the black land with the Nile waters. The king as the god Osiris unified the forces of nature and supernature, ensuring the annual flood of the Nile. (In his role as Scorpion he also saw to the digging of irrigation channels which conducted the Nile water to the farming plots.) He also measured time and the land, thus concentrating control of the calendar in the royal office.

The entire arable land was the king's domain. In bad times he fed his people from the state granary: the conjunction, in the early state, of the civil and ecclesiastic regime, is affirmed by the close relation of granary control and divine power.

Misfortunes and disasters were laid at the king's door; his physical powers and the well-being of the land were considered to be perfectly interlocked; and hence the ritual regicide. It should be noted, however, that regicide was not motivated by feelings of vengeance or protest; rather, it was an act of veneration so that the king might guide and maintain his worshipful subjects from beyond the grave, once again in his full power.

The Egyptian monarchy maintained a symbolic control over functions delegated to the ministries. While the royal office divided and distributed bureaucratic functions among the ministerial offices, the symbolic representation of those ministerial functions was retained in the titles and honors of the king: though agriculture was administered by an office charged with that function, the pharaoh was in himself Osiris, the god of the rebirth of the grain.

Egypt had been formed into an empire by internal political combination, including forceful conquest, and by foreign conquest. Prior to the political unification of Egypt under the pharaohs there had been many peoples, many ethnic unities—but there was no single term for the entire realm. The political identity of Egypt was established by the formation of the state; the ethnic identity of the Egyptian people emerged out of the political identity of the Egyptian state. This is a secondary process of formation of a popular unity, and of an ethnic identity, by a state organization. (This process was imperfectly developed in Ankole, for the agricultural Bairu were not embraced in an ethnic unity with the pastoral Bahima. But the process of ethnic identity correlative with a state formation *was* achieved by medieval Slavic and Mongol peoples, as we will show in chapters to follow. The Russians and other Slavic states, and the Mongols and other Tatar states, were formed on a newly emergent popular base. These peoples had not existed with these names and identities prior to the formation of the states which ruled over them.)

State Formation

Primary and Secondary
Delegation of Power

Émile Durkheim is responsible for the view that the unity of a social group is expressed in its ritual acts; that religion represents the sense of collectivity of the group. The unity of the complex society of Egypt, composed as it was of many territorial and class divisions, was expressed by a ritual of the god-king. The concentration of authority in a single head, at once secular and divine, was expressed in the cult of kingship and state, in which the absolute power of the kingship as secular ruler was the subject of veneration. Attribution of divinity made the kingship eternal, stable, and powerful as myth: the unity of the social whole was thrown back to an immemorial past and projected into an unending future. The central power of royalty in Egypt was the meeting place of the two realms—supernatural and earthly—over which the divine-king ruled; of the two realms of Upper and Lower Egypt; and of the line of temporal continuity of Egyptian society past, present, and future.

Both Shilluk and Egyptian kingdoms were ruled by sacred personages, the royal court and supporters being on a higher social plane than the common people. But local chiefs of the Shilluk never delegated their power wholly to the king, and so the king did not acquire all his power from the people. The pharaonic power *was* wholly delegated in his regime, and it was great; whereat he parsed and divided it. But Egypt was a state, and Shilluk was not.

Following the theory of Durkheim, ritual kingship also is the representation, in the religion, of the unity of the people under the throne. Local chiefs did not separate and allocate their power nor vest it in an integral royal body, or office of the central authority. Yet in the societies with merely ritual kingship and in societies with real temporal authority, the integral role of the symbolic center is similar. The formation of the supreme central authority is the expression of the political power of the social whole. Acknowledgment and support of this central authority is the primary act of delegation of political power of the social whole to the royal office, and such was the case in ancient Egypt. This was a ritual and civil rite, just as the office was both a ritual and civil office. Here was an early step in the formation of the state.

But this primary act of delegation of power into the hands of a central authority did not always take place, even within a unified polity. The League of the Iroquois, for example, had a supreme council with the power to make decisions concerning peace and war. However, it was not an independent body, but a dependent one. It was composed of delegates from councils of each of the five nations of the Iroquois League. The councils of each tribe or nation within the League reserved the right of veto over the supreme council; the supreme council of the League could not convene itself. The Iroquois case is an instance of failure by the society as a whole to assign and focus the primary power. The Iroquois League was not a state.

In the process of state formation the primary act of delegation of political power on the part of the social whole to the central authority is followed by a secondary act: the delegation of specific areas of authority by the king— the establishment of offices. Primary and secondary delegation go hand-in-hand; where there has been no fully developed primary delegation, then there is no secondary delegation, and vice versa. There was no central power in Kpelle, for it was polarized between the kingship and the head of the Poro, while in Shilluk there was no independent secular authority at all.

The central power of Ankole lay in the office of the king, which had no rival. The king of Ankole delegated one sort of power to his favorite chief; the border chiefs had their defense areas; personal followers in the court had their own civil and religious functions. Authority to act within limited spheres was doubly delegated in Ankole—gathered in the royal office, then distributed through lesser offices.

The pharaoh at first delegated his power only within the household, but later, secondary delegation was separated from the royal entourage. During the late predynastic and early dynastic periods, the king first secured his mandated authority, then separated the several functions which he performed. The royal office had grown complex, the geographic extent of rule had grown, the duties had increased. The conduct of the state ritual was delegated to a high priest; the affairs of the treasury were put into the hands of a treasurer; the office of curing was in the hands of a medical personage. In the combination of primary and secondary delegation of power lies the actual formation of the state; the anatomy of the state is the combination of functions and offices which the central authority has separated and delegated to ministers.

Separation of offices existed only after the royal power was established, not before. The offices of treasurer, high priest, military commander, did not elect or delegate a central authority. On the contrary, a monarch was confirmed in his office by representatives of tribes, village communities, and other social unities. For this reason, Meyer and Moret proposed that Scorpion in the pharaoh's title signified a tribe or community which came under the Egyptian power, the scorpion being the fetish of that tribe.

Max Weber held that Egypt was the earliest state with a bureaucratic administration. This is true, for Egypt was among the earliest states ever formed, and, in the meaning proposed here, all states have some element of bureaucratic organization in their various offices. Because evidence in writing is early in Egypt, we know of bureaucratic establishments and functioning. Waterworks and waterways were controlled by state offices as a requirement in the large-scale economy of the land, just as in ancient China, India, Peru, and Mexico. Likewise, maintenance of records rested partly in clerical and partly in secular hands, a vital function in the state apparatus from earliest times.

As Steward has shown, the state and its undertakings are large-scale as compared to societies without the state. Fortes and Evans-Pritchard pointed out that societies whose governments have the form of states are more populous than those which do not. For economy of effort and continuity of function, records are necessary in large enterprises. Indeed, most large-scale enterprises cannot work at all without written records.

The Egyptian state bureaucracy was established, as all others, by delegation of authority to offices with limited functions. Great bureaucracy, such as in the despotic powers of the ancient orient and in modern times, or small bureaucracy, such as in ancient Greece, is a proper part of the state.

In Egypt, the royal ritual and the state ritual were one; thus the unity of the people as a religious representation was given political expression: the representation of their political unity under the state. The state power had to be a legitimate one, conforming to the beliefs and customs of the people; the state power was affirmed as legitimate in the state ritual: coronation of the king, inauguration of the president. The ritual of the state expressed the myth of the founding of the state; the founding act was a myth, the subject of popular belief. This act was the principle which made legitimate the rule of the state. The doctrine of the Egyptian state is in fact that of the nation-state today.

The people in a society legitimate the sovereign power; the sovereign power is derived from the people who participate in the ritual act of legitimation when a new sovereign assumes the office. There is nothing false about this myth and its ritual expression; they refer to the constitution of the people in the state. "The myth," to paraphrase Malinowski, "is the founding charter of the state." Moreover, the social-contract idea current in the seventeenth and eighteenth centuries is itself a myth of legitimation of the state. According to this myth, individuals by contract gave up their perfect freedom in exchange for benefits from common life in civil society. This is not a foolish fancy; it is understandable as a myth of the origin of the state.

The state itself has acquired a myth of power, endowed with a (mythical) will of its own, and is often an object of worship. Those who adore power for itself venerate the state, and create thereby a cult of the state. Instead of a mode of relations as among human beings, the state then is made into a thing unto itself, with an existence independent of those who particate in it. This is the curious fallacy of reification: worshipers of state power have reified the state as cult by making it into a thing.

Five The Slavs

Slavic peoples today are divided by language into three main groups: eastern, western, and southern. The eastern Slavic group includes Russian, Ukrainian, and Belo-Russian; western Slavic includes Polish, Czech, Slovak, and small enclaves in Germany of Sorb or Wend; southern Slavic includes Bulgarian, Serbian, Croatian, Slovene, and Macedonian. Slavic was reduced to writing in the ninth century A.D., and it is at this relatively late time (other Indo-European languages having already been written for hundreds or even thousands of years) that the precise relations of the different Slavic languages to each other become clear to us.

Slavic unity of language was preserved down to the eighth and ninth centuries. The disruption of the primeval Slavic cultural unity, the invention and adaptation of their writing, deepening contact with Mediterranean civilization, and conversion to Christianity, were concurrent trends. Mediterranean civilization meant for the eastern Slavs primarily the political center of the Byzantine Empire, Constantinople; for the western Slavs, Rome; and for the southern Slavs both.

The Slavic World

The Slavs have lived for thousands of years in their central and eastern European habitat by clearing the surrounding forests and raising grain on the land. They have also raised farm animals, both for food and clothing and for animal power in the farm villages. And they have gathered the bounty of the surrounding country: water and fish from the streams; honey from the hives of wild bees; mushrooms, timber, furs, and meat from the flora and fauna of the forests; and metals, clay, and fuel from the earth.

The Slavs were not separate peoples and languages as we know them today, at least not until the first millennium of our era. Slavs are first mentioned by Roman and Greek writers in classical times. The picture they show is that of a simple folk not possessing a state structure. (The development of the state among Yugoslavs, Poles, and Russians at first followed the same course, as we shall see. We will pay attention particularly to the Russian state because there the early princes had much to say about their monopoly of power.)

The Earliest Record: Tacitus

In the first century A.D., Slavs were mentioned by the Roman historian, Tacitus, who paid some attention to details of their culture. He served as a Roman official in Germany in A.D. 89–93, and recorded that the Veneti, now known to have been the Slavs, lived in the forests and mountains between the Germans and the Finns—that is, on the southern shore of the Baltic Sea. They lived a wandering life, traveling swiftly on foot. They had settled habitations and supported themselves by raiding, reported Tacitus, who contrasted the movement of the Slavs with that of the mounted Sarmatians.[1]

Slavic culture is carried back further by archaeology, before the earliest written records, to the Bronze Age cultures in the second millennium B.C. By the study of human remains, similarities in bone structure of the inhabitants of the region have been traced from the Bronze Age down to historical times.

Slavic territory, evidenced by study of stone and bone remains, was comprised of the river valleys of the Oder and Vistula in Poland, possibly east of the middle course of the Dnepr in western Russia. There is a difference of opinion among specialists regarding the territorial location of Bronze Age cultures in the second millennium B.C. which are later identified as proto-Slavic. The Polish school has concluded, on the basis of remains of material culture (dwellings, tools, weapons) and skeletons associated with the cultural remains, that the forerunners of the early Slavic culture lived within the present boundaries of Poland. The Russian school has added the river valleys of western Russia to the territory of the forerunners of the Slavic culture.

[1] Tacitus, *Germania*, Chapter 46.

Tacitus' account of the life of the early Veneti accords well with the archaeological record. The early Slavs were settled in forest villages along the valleys of streams; they practiced a primitive form of agriculture, and knew the use of metals for tools and warlike weapons. It should be noted that the ethnic name Veneti appears ever again in reference to Slavic peoples. (Slavic peoples include the *Wends*, whose name is probably the same as that of the *Veneti*.)

The Slavs 2,000 years ago were in contact with Germanic peoples, Finns, and Iranians. They had but little contact with Rome, or with the eastern Mediterranean world. Tacitus probably saw little of the Veneti, if anything at all. He thought they might have been Germans or possibly Sarmatians (Iranians). But Slavic would have been unintelligible to either Germans or Iranians. There is no evidence of a state among these Slavs; on the contrary, their social organization was simple.

Slavs at the Close
of Classical Antiquity

By the sixth century A.D. the Turks—among them Huns, Avars, and Bulgars—appeared in strength beside the earlier settlers in eastern Europe. Byzantium was in close contact with Slavs, Germans, Iranians, Turks; contact was sometimes peaceful (trading goods, communicating ideas), sometimes belligerent (raiding, warring, taking slaves). These peoples combined with each other against Byzantium, or were allied with Byzantium in various combinations against each other. Consequently, reports varying in opinion as well as content were made by Byzantine and Roman writers concerning Germanic Goths, Slavs, and Turks. The most detailed of these accounts is by Procopios of Caesarea.

In the sixth century Procopios remarked that in ancient times the Slavs had been called *spori* (scattered), meaning that they had lived in separated or dispersed settlements, and therefore needed much land. In *De bello gothico (On the Gothic War)*, he wrote of the Slavs' simple social order. They were not governed by individual rulers but, as of old, lived under popular rule, sharing good and ill fortune in common. His judgment of the social system either bore upon an era long before his day, or else was a stereotyped expression of the life of the people. Probably it was a stereotype, for Procopios wrote that Roman slaves captured in battle had been owned by individual Slavic captors. There is no thought in these passages (regarding the disposition of slaves) of good fortune shared in common by all; the fortune in the person of the slave was privately acquired and owned. One slave, who had been a military leader when captured by the Sclaveni (Slavs), in fact served one master and fought bravely for him.

There is no doubt that the Slavs were, at the time, slave-takers and slave-owners. The question is: Were the Slavs private individuals and property owners, or did they live in a state of primitive communism in which all property was held in common? Procopios felt that, being backward compared to the Byzantine civilization, the Slavs must have lived as primitives—that is, communally. But his own texts disprove his view. The importance of the issue of private versus communal property is twofold; by its analysis and explication we gain both a better view of Slavic society and economy of that day, and an insight into the primitivist viewpoints of Byzantine writers (whose prejudices are not too different from our own). There can be no thought of primitive communism or primitivism among the Slavs of that time, even though they had no great cities such as Byzantium.

Procopios described the life of the early Slavs in the following terms:

> They reckon that there is but one god, the master of thunder, lord of all. To him they sacrifice bulls and have other sacred rites. They have no knowledge of fate and in general do not recognize that fate has any power over people. When death threatens in illness or in a position of danger in battle, they vow to sacrifice to the god if they are saved. Escaping death they make the avowed sacrifice and believe that their salvation was acquired at the cost of the sacrifice. They venerate rivers, nymphs, and other deities, sacrifice to them and by means of these sacrifices prophesy the future. They live in miserable huts, far removed from one another, and all of them change their habitations. In battle, they fall upon the enemy with shields and darts in hand; of armor they have none. Others have no chiton, nor cloak, but only trousers supported by a broad belt around the hips, and thus address the enemy. Among all these is a common tongue, all barbaric. In external appearance they are alike. They are very tall and strong. Their skin color and hair are fair or golden, not black. . . . Their life is rough, without favor, like the Massagetae; they are always covered with filth, but they are not evil nor wicked. . . .

The religion of these early Slavs was a polytheistic one, the chief god, whose name was Perun, being the thunder and sky god. As such, his features were shared by master deities of other Indo-European speaking peoples: Zeus of the Greeks, Jupiter of the Romans, Thor of the Germanic peoples. In their cult they worshiped river and forest deities; they sought by divination to foretell the future; and they sacrificed bulls (as did the Greeks). They did not believe in inescapable fate, but held that danger and evil could be averted by vows and sacrifices. They were optimistic about the chances of human intervention in determining their future, and so in this sense were the opposite of fatalistic. There is no mention of idols, nor of an organized priesthood. Even the role of the chief or king in the cult was much like everyone else's; indeed, it appears that in their comportment, Slavic rulers and their families were no different from common folk.

Tacitus remarked of the Slavs that although they were a wandering people, they had fixed habitations. The archaeological record provides an explanation for this seemingly self-contradictory comment. the Slavs' agriculture was of a type called *slash-and-burn*. Slavic territory was thickly forested, and the occupants felled and burned down trees to clear the ground, providing at the same time a primitive fertilizer for the soil. They may have known something of the soil fertilizing action of the ashes, for slash-and-burn had been practiced in northern Europe for thousands of years. In this type of agriculture the tillage plot is shifted after a few years, the settlement is moved to a new site, and the forest takes over the old. In Poland, slash-and-burn gave way to permanent agricultural settlement in the ninth century A.D.

Procopios noted that the Slavs lived in miserable huts, unlike the great edifices of the Mediterranean world to which the author was used. Slavic rulers' seats, he thought, were woefully poor by comparison with Byzantine palaces. But Procopios also wrote that in spite of the fact that they were filthy, the Slavs were nevertheless honorable—features of the "noble savage" idea discernible over many centuries in European and Oriental writings. Perhaps Procopios intended a criticism of the customs of his own people, who, though "civilized," were guilty of so much trickery and mendacity that he preferred the Slavic character—"uncivilized" but noble. Although Procopios' stereotyped writing must be regarded with caution, in most other respects his word is reliable. (See the discussion of "primitive communism," pp. 66–67.)

Combining what we have learned from historians such as Procopios and from archaeology, we may say the following of Slavic village and town life. These early Slavs lived in settled villages laid out along streams, in huts of wood daubed with clay. Their villages and towns had walls (formed by tree trunks laid laterally in place) within the confines of which cattle and stores of grain were kept. Defense of the settlements lay, aside from their walls, in their location, which was deep in their nearly impassible forests and swamps. The towns (which, it should be increasingly clear, were poor things compared with the Mediterranean and Oriental cities of that time) were concerned with civil affairs, rulership, and foreign trade, but the territories ruled from the towns are not always known to have had definite boundaries.

Usually the word "tribe" is attributed to the social system of the Slavs of this period. The term in Latin used by the writers of that time was *natio* (from which the word *nation* is derived). Originally, it meant "birth," and alluded to a social order of ties of common descent and consanguinity. But the term had changed its meaning and in the sixth century had reference to people of the place or territory. Slavic groups were identified by name of their descent group (*familia*) and by the locality in which they lived.

Central rule could only have been sporadic and ephemeral among the early Slavs; Roman and Byzantine writers were attuned to the presence of leaders, and they rarely mentioned leaders among the early Slavs. Although, as Mediterranean records indicate, the Slavs did not have kings, Slavic nobility increased in firmness of composition, in social differentiation from the common folk, and in wealth and substance at this time.

Historical records of the time tell mainly of wars between Slavs and Byzantium, Turks, and Goths; the archaeological record based on excavations indicates increasing trade relations between central, eastern, and northern Europe, and the eastern Mediterranean (the Slavs occupied settlements along rivers which were avenues of commerce). In addition, the circulation of economic goods supported political and military activities of Byzantium, the Avars and Huns, Goths and Slavs: gifts, counter-gifts, tribute payments, and offerings were a part of the political and economic system of the time.

During the seventh and eighth centuries Slavs continued to settle, both by peaceful means and by force, in the Balkans. They spread from their traditional area of western and southern Russia to central and northern Russia, and established new settlements in Poland and Czechoslovakia. They deepened spiritual as well as economic contact with the Mediterranean world. Towns expanded, and their functions as trade, administrative, and religious centers proliferated. Internal political stability depended on the power of their princes to lead in attack and defense; political stability was deepened by increase of wealth within the society by internal artisanry and trade. This wealth found its way into the hands of the rulers and nobility, whose power to rule was thereby reinforced.

Urban centers grew in wealth and power; trade with the eastern Mediterranean increased. The Norse traders came to the eastern Slavic centers to trade, and moved through Slavic territories along the river routes to the Black Sea and Byzantium. Eastern Slavic towns arose in the north, beside streams which flowed into the Baltic Sea, and other towns grew up by streams that flowed into the Black Sea, and along the Volga. Thus it is seen that Russian culture, territory, and polity were laid down even at that early time.

The Ninth Century: A Time of Transition

In the ninth century, the political structure of the Slavs took shape as firm and durable polities with centralized rule, class divisions, territorial definition, and written laws. Each nation had its own culture; nation and cultural unity became closely correlated.

Joseph Marquart (see Selected References) has called attention to the hundred-year period 840–940 in the peopling and national formations of parts of Europe and Asia. Ethnic and political composition was stabilized; a new state order was established. Peoples settled down; a new order of states was founded on new ethnic bases: the operational word is *ethnic*, and connected with it, *nation*, and *national*. This is in sharp contrast to the preceding polyglot empires. The national idea of territorial rights to be defended by armed might, and national consciousness of the different peoples, emerged in that epoch a thousand years ago. This idea has continued without interruption down to the present. Ethnic, national, and cultural identity were one, or at least tended to become one.

In the ninth century, territorial claims were asserted within the framework of the new monarchic polities. The peoples adhered to words, banners, and other symbols of their ethnic identity and difference from neighboring peoples. Christianity and the alphabet were now introduced by priests, and were not to be relinquished.

Conquest and Indigenous Slavic States

At least one Slavic state was formed by a conquest (of sorts): before the seventh century A.D., Slavic peoples settled in what is today Bulgaria, in the Balkans. But they were not immediately known as Bulgars, because at that time that name applied to a Turk-speaking people who lived along the lower Volga River. These Turkish Bulgars in turn migrated to Bulgaria in the Balkans, conquered the Slavic inhabitants, and ruled over them. The Turkish

Bulgar conquerors had a complex social order ruled by a king, or *khan,* and by nobles under him. In time, these Turks took on the customs and language of the people they conquered, and eventually became Christian converts. Within 300 years—that is, by the tenth century—they had lost their original culture, the only trace of which is in the name they brought with them, and which became that of the country they conquered.

Other Slavic nations—Serbs and Croats of Yugoslavia, and Poles of Poland—also formed their own states, both peacefully and by means of war. (At times their central authorities conquered neighboring peoples of similar cultural background and language to form their states.) In the process, they developed not only clear territorial boundaries and political independence, but a firm division between social classes, and a centralized office of rulership. During their development, these peoples increased foreign commerce and specialization in manufacture and trade.

The Slavs of the period before the ninth century show little evidence of these developments. Their leaders were not great central figures who were assured of a following and succession. On the contrary, their political confederations came and went, sometimes without trace. Therefore we know that we are dealing with peoples in transition from a stateless form of social organization to a state form. One office in the early history of the Serbs and Croats of Yugoslavia is a good example of the process of affirmation of rulership and of state formation. The Slavic titleholder of this office was the *Zhupan,* and the territory over which he ruled was called the *zhupa.* (The zhupa has been erroneously thought to be a tribe, and the *Zhupan* a tribal chief.) We shall momentarily discuss these terms further, as shown in the following quotation.

Serbs and Croats lived north of the Carpathians, between the Vistula and the middle Dnestr rivers, some time before the tenth century. An Arab writer of that time, Ibn Rusta, wrote:

> The land of the Slavs is a flat and forested land. Here they live and have neither vineyards nor sown fields. . . . They have few packhorses, and only prominent men have mounts. Their weapons are javelins, shields, and lances; other weapons they have none. Their prince is crowned, and they obey his word. His seat is in the midst of the Slavic land. The most famed and celebrated ruler, bearing the style of king of kings, is called Swet malik. He is mightier than the *supanj,* who is his representative.

The *supanj* (*Zhupan*) was the king's representative, a governor or district chief. The report of scarcity of Slavic horses, and the details of Slavic weapons, are consistent with the words of Tacitus and Procopios, and with the findings of archaeology. Slavs practiced slash-and-burn tillage totally different from the agriculture known to the Arabs. The Arabic record leaves no doubt that the *Zhupan* was an administrative aide in a political system of at least moderate complexity.

Serbs and Croats formed quasi-independent polities (*zhupas*) in the erstwhile Roman and Byzantine provinces of the Balkans during the eighth to tenth centuries. These provinces, then in Slavic hands, had no supreme rulers save, in a general way, the Roman or Byzantine emperors; a mythical supreme authority lay outside the Slavic domains, in Rome or Constantinople. Local lords (the aforementioned *Zhupans*) ruled over the *zhupas*, which were small territories in river valleys. Frontiers between *zhupas* were not fixed lines, but no-man's-lands—uninhabited forest or mountain zones. *Zhupas* were complex units, forming part of an international political system. The inhabitants were subjects of their lord, not to any significant degree or in any particular way his kinsmen.

The character of Balkan society had changed by the ninth and tenth centuries, and it is not to the point to think of a system of tribes. (In a similar way, *natio* had been separated from its original meaning of "unit" or "descent" or "common birth.") The Serbian *zhupas*, though still subject or tributary in an ill-defined manner to the eastern Roman Empire, were in a gradual process of forming a polity of their own. The lords were their own military leaders, judges, foreign ministers; there is no record that they delegated any of their functions. Their headquarters were located within a walled town or upon a fortified hill, and there they kept their ancestral seats or thrones. Administration of the fortified capital and the villages which together formed the *zhupas* was organized simply: elders conducted the affairs of their localities, and were responsible for them to their lord. Thus the traditional and the changing in the social life were combined.

The focus of political power over parts of Yugoslavia lay in Byzantium and Rome in the ninth century. Roman influence was concentrated on the Adriatic coast and islands; Byzantine influence was exerted from the east and south. Serbs now sided with Rome, now with the Eastern, or Byzantine, Empire. Local rulers were relatively independent in their choice of overlords, and on occasion were free of both.

The *Zhupans* gradually increased their independence during the ninth century because the hold of Rome and Byzantium had weakened due to commitments and setbacks elsewhere; and at the beginning of the tenth century a great *Zhupan* emerged in Serbia: Petar Goynikovich, whose rule extended over northern Montenegro and Herzegovina. Unifying the indigenous Serbian tribes, he founded a modest state with centralized power.

During the tenth to twelfth centuries, petty princes and dynasties arose, allied, divided, joined Byzantium, split away. Villagers were transformed into subjects of domains extending beyond the community of kinsmen and local lords. Crafts were further developed as architecture, metallurgy, and pottery techniques were improved. Roman influence in handicrafts was felt in Croatia, and Byzantine influence in Serbia. Social distance between nobility and commoners widened and deepened, and the political power of the nobility was strengthened. Local princes established their political centers near the commercial towns. Some achieved the power and ritual status of kings, wielding power to appoint clergy and a service (appointed by the prince) nobility who would be loyal to the throne. Serbs and Croats—as we have said—evolved their own states, which were of relatively homogeneous ethnic composition, ruled by indigenous overlords. Internal links and ranks of society were re-formed: traditional tribal formations were replaced by a state. Ties of blood and locality were replaced by political subjugation to a ruler removed in social distance, whose power was exerted through underlings and intermediaries: sword bearers, tax collectors, tributaries of the king; local nobility who depended on the royal bounty for their sustenance; and the service nobility—the aforementioned clients of the king who were his personal bondmen.

The *zhupa* territories of the southern Slavs eventually became the nuclei of the states, fixed in territorial bounds and stable in government. In the ninth to twelfth centuries, these were originally provinces or counties, then dependent or independent principalities. Their rulers evolved from local governors (administering their territory together with the community elders) to princes.

Similar processes are seen at work in ancient Poland. An attempt to establish an integral and central rule in the seventh century was short-lived, but the attempt and others like it had their effect in the next several centuries. Petty princes set up rule in small centers; little towns became centers of trade, manufacture, political administration, and military activity. Towns grew in size and their defenses were improved; for example, new walls and ramparts were built thicker and higher than the old, and troops were now mounted. (Animal figures were shown on town walls, not for decoration but as a ritual scene, part of the defense, for the people believed in the power of the ritualistic animals as emblems.) Satellite towns and villages were incorporated around these centers, and peasants tilled the surrounding land. Iron and silver were locally mined, and worked by smiths in the towns. In this period agriculture was changed from primitive slash-and-burn to the permanent, settled, arable system of the present day. Trade with the Mediterranean and Arab lands was increased. The political centers proceeded with the internal conquest of Poland.

Early rulers are dimly referred to in legends and myths (one of them is supposed to have been eaten by rodents). The first genuinely historical Polish king, accounted the founder of the Polish state, ruled from 960 to 992; his seat of government was Poznan. At this point we observe a transformation of history from legend to objective record, although in fact the history is a continuum, the legendary and objective both serving the same purposes: recording events and affirming the moral meaning popularly assigned to them. Thus their history serves a dual purpose, as record and as myth. (Bronislaw Malinowski has pointed out this dual role in regard to the Trobriand Islanders of the southwest Pacific, and Meyer Fortes in regard to the Tallensi of West Africa.) But the early Polish record is one-sided: we only have the ruling, the official view. The content of the record, the process of its transmission, and the message which it is intended to convey are parallel to those of the rulers of ancient Egypt and other early states—it is not that of the common folk, whose record is missing.

The Rus of Kiev

The Ukraine is a flat country crossed by broad rivers which flow into the Black Sea. It is forested along its river valleys, where neolithic farmers once tilled the soil, but otherwise is sparsely populated with trees. Its soil is rich and black; the land is well-drained; its natural plant cover is the grassy vegetation of the lush steppe, which here grows thick and high when left undisturbed. Today the Ukrainian steppe is largely farmland, supporting wheat, rye, barley, maize, legumes—though cattle and other livestock still are raised here, as they have been since nomads first tended their flocks and herds on this abundant flatland.

The Ukrainian capital is Kiev, a great city at the confluence of the Dnepr and Desna rivers. Here an early Slavic state was formed, which was certainly in existence in the ninth century of our era. Sporadic but notable polities were formed by eastern Slavs in the Ukraine and southern Russia at various times in the first millennium A.D. These various political enterprises were not states, properly speaking, but *proto-states*, consisting of short-lived but independent, integral regimes with a central authority dominating over a complex, stratified social order. An example is the fourth-century principality of the Slavic Antes ruled by king (or prince) Boz. The social and ritual distance between rulers and ruled was perceptible to outsiders; the domain of rule had an internationally recognized identity. However, these polities lacked internal stability; they often collapsed under attack, and either were not reconstituted at all, or else were reconstituted under new and different regimes, without popular consciousness of continuity or fidelity.

Norsemen trading with Slavs and Byzantium allied with these countries, serving with and under them in war. During the middle of the ninth century they had moved from beyond the Baltic (or Varangian) Sea and into the territory of the eastern Slavs in some force, and there they remained. These Norsemen were called *Varangians*, or *Rus*, and were collectively identified by their Slavic hosts as merchants.

Origin of Rus

The term *Rus* is the root of the word for Russia; its early meanings tend to be confusing, and only in their clarification can something of the international and interethnic relations of their times be understood. Some medieval texts clearly refer to the Norsemen—other texts to the Slavs—as Rus. A Slavic record of the early tenth century describes the enactment of a treaty between Greeks and Rus. The Greek party, being Christian, affirmed the treaty by kissing the cross, but the Rus, who were heathen, swore according to their law: upon their weapons, by their god Perun, and by Volos, their cattle god. These were not Norse or Germanic gods, but Slavic gods; the Rus here are Slavs. Again, however, a certain Prince Oleg ruled over Varangians, Slavs, and others, who were *all* called Rus in the ninth century. The varying usages point to a generality: that "Rus," to the Greeks and Slavs, meant a country in which different ethnic groups lived. The country was under the rule of the Varangians, the indigenous population was eastern Slavic, and there were others, perhaps Finns and Balts, in the country. Greeks identified the various ethnic groups by the land from which they came, but the Slavs also used the term Rus to designate the Varangians specifically. The term for the entire land and the various peoples in it was taken from the name for the Varangians.

The Czech scholar T. G. Masaryk, founder of the Czechoslovakian Republic, conceived of the Russian state as having been formed out of the political organization introduced by neighboring civilizations, Norse to the north and Byzantine to the south. However, we must first deal with the *indigenous* forces of development of the Russian state, in interchange with the external factors mentioned. Nothing is made of nothing: if a people has not developed to the point of state formation, that formation cannot be superimposed. The Russians had a modest political development with state form of rule by the ninth century; they further developed this in that century and later on, during a period of increasing foreign contact.

Monkish chroniclers writing in the eastern Slavic language and script described the Norse and Slavic social organization and their relations to each other. The Slavic peoples, as we are told, invited the Norsemen to rule over them, pointing out that their land was rich but unruly, and in need of government. Three brothers, with their families and retainers, came to the east, to Rus. They settled in the north and south, and in Kiev. In coming to rule in Kiev they encountered other Varangians, whom they told, "You are not princes, nor of princely house. But [we are] of princely house." (The term for house was *rod*, which at that time meant family, house, patriline, those related in the patriline, and social position by right of birth in the patriline, and covers many of the same connotations as *natio*.)

Social and Political Organization

Both the Slavs and the Norse had a complex social organization composed of higher and lower social strata. Both ethnic groups had already developed a central ruling house and royal line. The eastern Slavs had developed the idea of central rule over a complex society, composed of various social estates and ethnic groups with a fixed territory. The Norsemen were not bound to a territorial organization, but to a personal relationship of follower and overlord—a master-client relation. Out of the combination of the two sets of social institutions the Russian state emerged.

Local Slavs and Norse, unified partly by force, fixed the capital at Kiev, and established relations with other states. Under the new rulership, Rus became a stable and permanent polity. Just as early attempts at forming states were fleeting before the definitive act of state formation, so Christianity was introduced briefly, only to disappear. It was not until a century later that Christianity was lastingly introduced into Russia. The formation of the state, and conversion to Christianity, were related; Christian doctrine contributed to the stability of the state, and Christian monks kept official records from the tenth century on.

The society of that day was organized according to law set forth, interpreted, and executed by the royal court. Although it applied indifferently to Norsemen and Slavs, it established distinctions between high and low estates, and levied fines and punishments accordingly. Outside the royal court, noblemen held patrimonial properties; lesser householders conducted their affairs in dependence on the central government. The tillers of the soil—freemen, bondmen, and slaves—were at the bottom of the pyramid. Merchants had an established place in the society alongside the landholders.

The royal court was composed of a bodyguard, court-appointed functionaries, landless noblemen, men-at-arms.

The Mediterranean cultures received reports concerning those eastern Slavs living in the area of the Black Sea and the Ukraine, and of those who lived in contact with the Baltic. Long before the ninth century, Slavs were also settled in the Volga region of central and northern Russia in considerable numbers and over a wide area. Here was a part of the Slavic world which prior to the ninth century was beyond the direct ken of the Mediterranean. Originally they existed in tribal formations; however, by the time of the eastern Slavic chronicles of the eleventh century, they were involved in the process of eastern Slavic political integration. Slavic peoples of south Russia had developed a number of sporadically instituted, nascent states or proto-states; those of the center and north of Russia may have had such, but nothing is known of this. Slavic townsmen of the Baltic region maintained their political and commercial independence; oriented to the Baltic trade, they were for centuries separate polities.

Slavic peoples of this time have been given tribal names, but this is an error. And although they continued to bear tribal names down to the historical period, the mere continuation of these names does not indicate the character of the societies. Most of these peoples had complex social structures—i.e., permanent divisions of society into higher and lower social orders, and a supreme ruler in whose hands the political authority over the people was concentrated. International relations were complex: governments treated with each other as equals, or as tributaries, or as dependents, or as subject to conquest and absorption. One people, the *Drevlyans*, were ruled by a prince named Mal. The Kievan prince Igor, on a military campaign against him to collect tribute on behalf of his state, was treacherously killed, his wife succeeding to the throne and avenging his death with acts of terror. Such acts bespeak a civilized and advanced political system as are recorded in the famous *Lay of the Host of Prince Igor*. On the other hand, Slavic peoples of the Volga region, far from Kiev and the events of the great world, were more primitive and simple in their social organization; they preserved a tribal system to a greater extent and long after the others.

There is another factor weighing against considering these medieval Slavs as tribes. Tribes as a rule are peoples of homogeneous culture within their territories; that is, such things as dress, household and agricultural implements, and dwelling and village settlement patterns are usually the same within a tribe, although differing from tribe to tribe. In recent times, archaeological parties have dug up ornaments, utensils, and other cultural remains, and certain types of ornaments and costumes from among these have been plotted on maps. But the maps of territorial and political divisions do not coincide with the maps showing where these remains were found. The impression given by these different mappings is definitely not that of a tribal system. The alternative explanation is that the peoples of Russia at that time were in the process of political recombination: they moved about, coming into contact with different peoples, changing their traditional ways, and changing names. There is a reservoir of names for peoples; names recur within the Slavic world, as we have seen. Some of the same names appear to have been drawn upon by several Slavic peoples in the process of their formation and re-formation.

Villages and Towns

The Slavs of Russia lived chiefly on the land, in villages alongside streams. Their towns were typically of wood, with wooden houses and a *paling*, or fence of wood, enclosing the entire town. The chief of these were centers of Baltic trade, such as Novgorod and Pskov, in addition to Kiev, the capital in the south, and Smolensk in the west of Russia. These cities were commercial and political centers, as well as centers of spiritual culture— vital factors in building the Russian state. Capitals, such as Kiev, provided a firm and stable location for the center of political power; they were a point of reference to all the people for all their activities. The prince in the political center asserted authority and exacted obedience. Taxes and tribute flowed into the center; when added to the accumulated riches of commerce, they helped create an urbanism which, in its wealth of architecture, ornament, dress, weaponry, transportation, and so on, far outshone the rest of the land. The capital became the measure of the greatness of the realm, of the power of the prince and of the people. The health and wealth of the princely court and of the capital town demonstrated the health and wealth of the entire land.

There were also towns which resisted further political pyramiding. The chief of these was Novgorod, which had a lucrative trading relation with northern and western Europe. They conducted their own affairs, led by an assembly of merchants and others of the propertied classes. On occasion, these towns combined with local nobility as political forces which counter- balanced the centripetal and monopolistic tendencies of princely and royal power. Thus the merchant cities assumed a role of considerable importance against the central state, at times encouraging the local nobility to similar action. The assembly, or *veche*, was widespread in Russia: in village assem- blies, just as in the towns, elders met, discussed their affairs, and made their decisions.

The Law Code

The ancient Russian code of criminal and constitutional law pro- vides a detailed picture of social stratification and custom, as well as of government, in the ninth-, tenth-, and eleventh-century Russia. According to criminal law, blood vengeance was generally acceptable: "If a man kills a man, then brother avenges brother; a son the father, or a father the son; the brother's son, or the sister's son." But the law also provided for circumstances under which blood vengeance either could not be carried out, or might not be appropriate. In such cases the payment of a *wergild*, blood money, was considered compensation for homicide: "If there is no one to avenge the dead, then forty silver pieces will be paid per head. . . . If he be a Rus, in the prince's bodyguard, or a merchant, court functionary, man-at-arms, or a nobleman without inheritance, one in attendance on the Grand Prince, or if he be a Slav, forty silver pieces will be set down for him" (Article I).

Other provisions of the code set forth punishment to be administered if property was stolen, if bondmen or slaves took flight, if a householder was killed by bandits. In the case of murder by bandits, the blood money was applied, and if the murderer was not found, then the blood money was paid by the community in which the victim was found (Article XX). (This community was neither a village nor a kin-community, but an administrative unit.) The blood money was collected from a district which was a formal part of the prince's domain, subject to his regulation. The central authority circumscribed the administrative areas and functions of the subordinate political units.

By examining this ancient law code, a rare insight is gained into the function of absolute monopoly of state power while the state is in process of formation. (One of the criteria for the formation of a state is the absolute monopoly of power, and the Russian princes, jealous of their power, divided it with none save those who served directly under them.) Thus, the law code states: "He who harms a peasant without the prince's word pays three pieces of silver fine for the wrong done, but he who harms a householder, or a prince's retainer, or man-at-arms, pays twelve pieces of silver" (Article XXXIII).

Although the law applied indifferently to Norsemen and Slavs, it did establish distinctions of estate: the fine for doing physical harm was assessed according to the station of the one harmed. Those of high estate were reckoned to be worth four times those of the low estate. Injury to a slave was too small to be reckoned, but injury to the prince was not reckoned, no punishment being too great. Stealing a slave from another man was assessed at the same rate as a physical injury done upon his person: twelve pieces of silver was the fine. In any case, no one had the right without express authority to harm a fellow subject other than a child, a slave, or a bondman of one's own; physical punishment lay in the hands of the central authority unless it was otherwise specifically delegated.

Russian society of that day was organized according to law set forth, interpreted, and executed by the royal court. The characteristic political and military institution which supported this state power was the retinue—personal servants, followers, and clients of the king (including landless noblemen, court-appointed functionaries, men-at-arms, a bodyguard, and sometimes even foreigners)—all of whom were no longer in any way bound to the people or territories of the king's rule. If they came from a locality of the king's domain, they abandoned their ties to it and undertook a bond to the person of the king—a personal relationship of fealty. Ties to locality were divisive forces; the personal bond, on the contrary, undergirded the central power. At the same time, however, the personal bond of the retinue to the king had an inherent weakness, which was introduced throughout Europe at the time: these were clients of the king, not of the throne or the realm or state. If the king was overthrown or died, or if his power and wealth were diminished, the royal retainers were quits with the kingdom, and in fact could not be counted on to support the royal succession. Indeed, with the decline of the personal prowess of the ruler—his impoverishment or death—the very retinue which had supported the tendency toward political centralization of the kingdom now contributed toward its dismemberment.

Throughout earlier times, wealthy and powerful landowners, only theoretically subordinate to the king, could live independently in their own manors—heavily fortified settlements where religious and civil records were maintained. However, during the tenth and eleventh centuries, the division of the land into patrimonial manorial estates, and the division of the people into social estates, progressed, and political and territorial unity became firmly established. The royal court and person became supreme; towns, rural manors, and royal retinue *all* became dependents of the king. Social division between nobility and commoners was established for the next thousand years. The upper stratum of society was divided into royalty and nobility; merchants were treated much as the landholders; commoners were divided into freemen (who usually tilled the soil), bondmen (serfs) bound to the soil, and slaves (personal property). The church, with its bishops and clerics, had its own hierarchy parallel to the secular arm. The tribal-consanguineal bond and the bond to the local territory was long since past, the character of the Russian state was finally established.

We have seen that the primary forces in this entire process of state formation were indigenous: the centralization of royal power, the growth of town and manors in wealth, and the development of the personal retinue of the king. This was truly a case of internal conquest—conquest, by an ever more centralized royal authority of fellow tribesmen and villagers, of related tribes, villages, districts, and provinces, and finally of tributaries. To all of these the culture and laws of the central regime inevitably were carried; of all of these was formed the state.

Nation-State and Folk

Nation-State

The nation-state of contemporary Europe emerged out of medieval patterns. The nation as an ethnic and cultural unity was the basis for the political unity under the medieval crown. The lesson that Marquart has taught is that the political state formation coordinated territorial unity, cultural unity, and ethnic unity, with consciousness of identity. This unity was shaped out of peoples in village communities who were partly or wholly prepared to accept the new political form, and who were made aware of relationships beyond the village; these relationships placed them in the lower social order, while the center of the wider social and political web lay far away and socially far above the village. Villages are segmentary, not hierarchical, organizations. In contrast, the state is a hierarchical type of social and political integration, spanning over many such communities. These communities must first be conjoined by economic interdependence, a process which is indicated archaeologically by increasing trade and improved technology; by political and military force imposed by the burgeoning center; by the needs for common defense; and by widening recognition of common cause and common culture among villages. The community must be integrated into the larger political entity by forces introduced from without the village world. The state power contravenes the village forces and embraces all villages in its territory.

Folk

The roots of the nation-state are partly embedded in the *folk,* and in its communal sentiment and orientation. But the communal, collective sentiment of the folk is a limited one, and is also anti-state. The Romantic thinkers, poets, and collectors of folklore of the nineteenth century idealized the folk and exaggerated the depth of its feeling as a collective whole. The peasant village opposes the state because its political structure is not in itself a proper part of the state and does not flow into the state smoothly; it is counterposed to the extensive, universalistic rule of the state. The peasant village is particularistic, as Weber put it, having one rule for its own members, another for outsiders; the village customary law asks who you are and applies the law depending on the answer. The law of the state is no respecter of persons and may not ask, in theory at least, who you are; it is applied with disregard to everyone, everywhere within its boundaries (in theory).

The Slavic states, one thousand years ago, were past the initial stages. Local loyalties had been overcome, and integrated rule had been established in many parts of eastern Europe. While steps were taken toward a central kingship from the fourth to the seventh centuries, only in the ninth and tenth centuries was the process of political integration put on a firm base: a Slavic system of writing was widely spread; Christianity was definitely implanted among the Slavs; Slavic cultural and linguistic unity was broken up and different Slavic languages achieved specific territorial definition; Slavic princes treated with Mediterranean and Germanic powers as co-equals.

The alphabet gave the reigning princes a means of governing great and complex political structures by maintaining records. Taxes were recorded, laws disseminated; all the business of the state was now in the hands of the central ruler and his offices and officers. As the alphabet, so religion: Christianity gave the Slavs access to a world religion, to worldwide movements of thought, both spiritual and technical; and it undergirded the rulers with a powerful mystique which went far beyond the bonds of place and custom. Islam and Judaism performed the same function among neighboring peoples, but Christianity was without rival among the Slavs. And it was Christian monks who introduced letters to the Slavs.

The gulf between lord and peasant widened and deepened. Peasants of various rank maintained various kinds of masters, as freemen, voluntary bondmen, involuntary bondmen, slaves. Peasants were bound by oath, debt, and forceful seizure; they became property early in the history of the state.

The Slavic states, as we have seen, were developed chiefly by internal processes, including internal conquest. Their subjects were in the main of monogeneous composition: Slavic. An exception, the Bulgarian state, was formed by superimposing a conquest dynasty of Turkish origin upon a Slavic population. The Kievan state of Rus was developed by combination of Norse-Varangians with indigenous Slavic merchants, rulers, and warriors. The Slavs of Kiev had a central political rule of their own, later mastered by the Norse-Varangians and integrated into the historical Rus state.

The Kievan state, according to its earliest records, established the monopoly of physical force in the hands of the highest political authority. Power to coerce by violence or threat of violence rested with none but the prince and his delegated officers. The explicit nature of this monopoly was expressed in the law; the importance of this to the study of the state formation cannot be overestimated. The law code was monopolistic in application: within the Kievan state no other law or custom was acknowledged.

The early princes of Kiev and Poland created personal bonds of fealty among a retinue of men who were their military arm and councilors—the fellowship, or *druzhina*. Since they were a personal following, they did not feel themselves bound to the state in general if their personal lord died or was overthrown, or slain in war. The personal bond of master and man has already been examined in the African cases cited: to a modest degree in Kpelle, to a greater degree in Ankole, and further among the Slavs. It will also be examined in Tatary.

The problem of overcoming local loyalties and of establishing a broader world-view for the local lords and peasantry was solved in their own way by the Slavic states. The military following became a serving nobility composed of noblemen while in the royal service, and of the ennobled as a reward for services. They were a counter-weight to the local nobility. Christianity, trade, taxation, and legal administration all bound the local communities to the central office of rulership. The village community and the manor of the local lord, or *boyar*, were the anvils upon which the state was hammered out.

The tribe had long since disappeared from eastern Europe, if by "tribe" we mean a small group of people with a common culture, lead by a chief who was barely differentiated from the tribe-folk. The tribal system was no longer in force when the Norsemen-Varangians came to Russia.

The passage from small political units to the system of states of east and southeast Europe was not a smooth continuity. The local allegiances to which the people were accustomed had to be broken. New allegiances, those to the central authority, were substituted; these comprised the religious-legal-economic system dominated by royal office and the state. The village community was finally integrated, often by force, into the larger whole. It never stood in perfect harmony with the central power; rather, it was a source of rebellious sentiment and indeed of rebellion for the next thousand years. The Russian *boyars* at first resisted the central power, but were brought around by the seventeenth century.

The Slavic states were formed in each case by integration of local life into a larger whole: a land dominated by a central court with international diplomatic, military, religious, and economic relations. But the new power structure was not always universal in its rule—that is, everywhere dominant within its territory: petty lords and princes, fortified in their great estates, were often obstreperous in their opposition. The merchant chiefs of the cities were also centers of opposition to the grand princes and kings.

The rulers of the early Slavic states were not grand monarchs. Throughout the Middle Ages they constantly wrestled with personal bonds of retainers, bonds which they sought to objectivize; these they sought to release from their persons and attach to their thrones. They were beleaguered by external enemies and local loyalties which were hardly, and only with difficulty, brought into the political system of the central state.

Six The Tatar State
Turks and Mongols

Early in the thirteenth century the Mongols, previously known to Europeans only as a terrible scourge sent from God, suddenly descended upon them. Conquering the Rus of Kiev, the invaders swept through eastern and central Europe, campaigning victoriously in Poland, eastern Germany, and the Danube valley. But then, inexplicably—and much to the relief of Rome, the Germans, the Poles, and the Hungarians—they retreated, retaining of Europe only their Russian dominions, which remained in their empire until the end of the fifteenth century. Viewed from within the Mongol polity, these hit-and-run activities were perfectly understandable, but to Europeans, who were not then well-informed about the Orient, they were long a matter for puzzled discussion. The Mongol Empire of the thirteenth and fourteenth centuries, the whys and wherefores of its modus operandi still largely shrouded in mystery, eventually extended from the Pacific Ocean across all of Asia, incorporating the Near East as far as the Mediterranean, and Russia, China and Persia inevitably fell to the Mongols, also, as did the lands of central and inner Asia.

82

The Tatar World

Mongolia, the Mongol homeland, is a high country, far from the oceans of the world. The terrain is desert in the south, steppe in the central latitudes, and steppe merging into Siberian forest in the north. The Mongols are pastoralists, subsisting on the products of domesticated sheep, goats, cattle, yaks, horses, and camels. They have no fixed residence, but nomadize with their herds in an annual round from pasture to pasture; their dwellings are portable tents of felt and cloth. As one might expect, hunting is their most important supplementary occupation.

A people called the *Huns* occupied the highland of Mongolia even before the Mongols did, and, just three centuries before our era, these pastoral nomads again made that country their home. A Chinese writing, which states that the Huns led a nomadic existence based on rearing herds of stock, also reports of these Huns, "Their country is the back of a horse." The Huns who inhabited Mongolia 2,300 years ago stood in close relations—now amicable, now bellicose—with the Chinese farmers to the south. Later, Turks succeeded each other in occupying the Tatar steppes, but their economy, their nomadic movement with mounts and carts for transport, their living arrangements in felt tents, and their relations with the Chinese, all were continuities of the Hun pattern of existence.

Relations to China

The Chinese a thousand years ago indiscriminately referred to the Turks and Mongols who occupied their northern marches as *Tatars*.[1] The Russians during the period from the thirteenth to the fifteenth century were ruled wholly or in part by Mongols and their Turkish allies and successors; to Russians this was the period of imposition of the Tatar yoke. Out of the Chinese and Russian usages has arisen agreement on the similarity of Mongol and pastoral Turkish culture and rule; this agreement is partially justified by the accord in their internal and external relations between nomadic Turks and Mongols. At the same time, of course, differences are to be noted—variations on a basic system-in-common.

Chinese farming had a great effect upon the economy of the steppes, since Chinese grain and textiles were exchanged and/or fought for by the nomads. Because steppe peoples did not grow their own farming produce, a monopoly of tea, rice, millet, wheat, cotton, and silk exchange lay with the Chinese. This monopolistic role of China had important consequences:

1. The steppe peoples turned to agriculture only when they moved westward, away from China.
2. The steppe peoples of various ethnic affiliations and periods concentrated on the herding economy in Mongolia.

---

[1] *Tatar* is also, it should be noted, the name of a nomadic group in Mongolia who early joined Chingis Khan's confederation.

3. The herders provided China with horses for cavalry, civil transport, communication, and leather; camels for transport; cattle for leather and meat; sheep and goats for wool, hides, and meat. Various animals acquired from the steppes worked on the Chinese agricultural plots. Bone, horn, and teeth provided China with tools, weapons, and medicines.
4. China provided the northern steppe barbarians with tea, cereal grains, and cloth of silk and cotton. The different products were circulated from one area to the other by trade and marketing conducted by public officials and private entrepreneurs. Public acts of tribute payment and collection were another vital part of the interchange.

The two cultures, of peasants and herdsmen, became mutually dependent, out of which a great symbiosis emerged. The Chinese farming and the Tatar pastoral cultures remained independent and distinct; at the same time, they were joined in a sort of continent-wide institutional web, or network. Part of this web was the economic exchange pattern, closely related to the systems of land use in China and the Tatar steppes. The Turks and Mongols came to rely on China for their agricultural needs, and did little farming on their own; north Chinese came to rely on the steppe peoples for their herding products. Agricultural land supports a dense population, in China more than in the other agricultural countries. By careful land management, irrigation, and marketing, Chinese agriculture is able to support a hundred times as many people per unit of ground as the Mongol and Turkish herdsmen can.

From the Chinese point of view, herding is a wasteful use of the soil: flocks and herds can extract only so much nourishment from any one area, and so must spread out thinly, circulating throughout the year among their pasturages. Herdsmen do not plant or tend the grasses on which their herds depend, or cultivate new pastureland; they rely on natural forces to replace the grass which their herds have cropped. Of course, since the amount of grass is limited, the number of livestock it can support is also limited. Size and density of herding populations are low compared with those of the Chinese farmers.

Trade versus Tribute

In trade and marketing, economic factors predominate in values and terms of exchange. Commodities traded have values which are determined by considerations internal to the market. Nomadic Mongols and Turks expressed the unit value of their herds in terms of the exchange value of a grown horse (*bodo*); sheep, camels, and cattle were worth so many horses. Then, in external exchange, the herd units had the value of so many bushels of rice, so many bricks of tea, so many bolts of cotton. In theory, past market transactions, current supply and demand, and pressures and pinch on individuals involved in the transaction, all determined the course of the bargaining.

In tribute payment and collection, on the other hand, the political and military strength and the nuisance value of the peoples are taken into consideration. Tribute is an official and public transaction, as between representatives of polities; trade may be either private or public. Tribute on the steppes was a two-way street; the more powerful in the tribute relation forced the weaker party to increase the amount in the exchange, while proffering less than usual from his side. Thus, if steppe peoples were strong, the Chinese increased the amount of rice, tea, silk, or cotton, and received fewer horses, sheep, camels, wool, or hides in return. If the Chinese were strong and the steppe peoples in turmoil, the Chinese appeared in force, with troops and with only a small counteroffering. These were large-scale movements of goods, and were carefully calculated—at least by the Chinese. The steppe peoples took advantage of border situations and raided at those points where the Chinese were weak. Thus, the exchange system frequently broke down and politico-military force took over in the relations between the steppe and farming cultures. Another consequence of these economic and political relations was that the steppe polity remained small in scale, and relatively simple, despite the proximity to China. China was the paramount high culture of eastern Asia, and is so to this day.

The institutional web was political and military as well as economic. Military factors entered in on more occasions than merely when normal exchange broke down: politico-military factors determined the tone and pace of economic relations, the values of goods in exchange, and the subordinate or superordinate status of those engaged in the exchange. This last relationship was made clear in a ritual ceremony, according to which the stronger party spoke first and the weaker offered tribute first.

Sumptuary wares (luxury items of the upper classes) were also exchanged, both in trade and in tribute. Turks and Mongols brought pelts of ermine, sable, bear, fox, and squirrel to the market and to the tribute offering; Chinese brought silk and jewels. These were valued as marks of status between the herdsmen and the Chinese representatives. The sequence of offerings and the value of the jewels and furs which were offered were calculated according to the participants' evaluation of the current standings of international relations. These sumptuary wares were at the same time marks of social distinction between the upper and lower strata, both in China and in Mongolia.

China, Tibet, and Mongolia were also joined in a religious institutional web, the primary component of which was Buddhism. Buddhist monasticism, both monks and monasteries, and Buddhist religious doctrines and rituals came to Mongolia from Tibet and China.

The peoples of the Tatar steppe are known from the first millennium B.C. From that time forward they maintained economic, political, military, and religious relationships with China. Although the steppe peoples were of various ethnic origins, earlier they were Turks, and latterly Mongols. The economy and the relation to the habitat of all these peoples was a stable one, and the tradition of pastoral nomadism in the Mongolian steppe persisted, regardless of the ethnic identity of the principal occupant at any time.

A number of factors contributed to the stability of the tradition. Turks and Mongols are related by language and culture; they share membership in the Altaic language family, which in addition to these components also includes Manchu-Tungus. Some of these moved off, and gradually developed distinctive cultures and sharply different languages. Turks and Mongols remained in contact in Mongolia and neighboring areas of central Asia, southern Siberia, and western China, thereby furthering their cultural similarities.

Habitat

The habitat of Mongolia is favorable to herding; the sheep, goats, horses, camels, and bovines have been found both wild and domesticated on the steppes, uplands, and drylands of Asia. Climate and terrain, the sumptuous grass carpet over vast pastures, and the water supply, all make possible the great herding enterprises of the people. Farming is also possible, but to have continuously successful farming year after year, the Turks and Mongols of that time and place needed different implements, seed, and tilling practices than they possessed. But the Turks, as they moved westward, came to parts of western Turkestan, Europe, the Caucasus, and Turkey, where they could develop farming techniques. Thus we see that the limitations placed on the development of farming in Mongolia, and the consequent concentration on herding there, were a result of the *cultural* environment (due largely to the proximity to and influence of China), and not of the limitations of the *natural* environment.

Turks and Mongols had stabilized their relations with the environment: the successive occupants of Mongolia were nomadic herdsmen, engaged in a set of institutional relations with China. These relations often broke down— the economic strands were but fragile, easily frayed. Poor harvests, internal dissensions, rebellious troops, and the like, all created Chinese border situations which the herdsmen used to their advantage, raiding rather than trading. In times of breakdown, the institutional web was a defective symbiosis between farmers and herdsmen; but it was one which has been undervalued, because it worked much of the time. The herdsmen in this context developed an increasingly complex form of government and army. Europeans were overwhelmed by a military force out of the steppes for which they were unprepared. But the Mongol conquests were the result of a sequence of internal developments which are to be explained here.

Social and Political Organization

During the past 2,000 years, inhabitants of the Mongolian steppe, whether Turk or Mongol, have been pastoral nomads whose social organization has been a uniform system. Mongols and Turks have also maintained a strongly masculine world-outlook: kinship and descent are reckoned in the male line; rights of inheritance of property and honors pass from father to son, brother to brother, paternal uncle to nephew; women come to live with their husbands' families. The orientation of the family lies in the raising of a son: the wife confirms her position in her husband's family, as well as her position in society, as the mother of a son. Men are the leaders of the family, the village, the clan, and the empire.

An ordinary pastoral village of nomads in Mongolia is usually arranged in the form of either a circle, or an arc, of tents. The basis of village organization is the extended family, composed of a patriarch and his sons, and their wives and children. Since families in the village are related, a kin community is formed. Typically, the entire village is descended from a common founding ancestor.

The history of the formation of these kin communities is directly related to the history of herding in Mongolia. In the past, the rich families with great herds could not move without making arrangements for their herds; therefore the leading herdsmen in the family, when dispersing for the summer pastures, were assisted by poorer herdsmen and those who entered as clients into their service. The rich families, then, with their many widespread kin, clients, and servants, originated the nomadic village community system; the leader of each community was the senior member of the leading local family. With the onset of winter, the communities combined to form great encampments. At this time, decisions were made concerning regulations of pastoral nomadizations for the next year, disputes were arbitrated, and the religious ritual of the village was conducted. Villages were grouped into *clans*, and clans further into *confederations*, all still related by bonds of descent from a common ancestor. Thus, all male members of a clan or a confederation were related, even if only distantly; emperor and subject might be tenth or twentieth cousins in the male line. Each clan had a body of ritual which was special unto itself: ceremonies venerating clan ancestors, clan spirits, territorial spirits, the natural forces and phenomena of the territory.

Nevertheless, this uniform kinship structure was divided into unequal estates, the nobility and the commoners. Both were estates related by descent from the clan founder; but in practice they were divided by differences in birth, wealth, accident, migrations, wars. Descent lines were not equal; the line of the firstborn was more highly placed than any other, having the right of seniority. The junior lines followed in order; the next in seniority succeeded to the highest place if the firstborn line was cut off without issue or with female issue, since a woman was held to be the end of her family.

Leadership was a status that was not assigned by rote—it had to be achieved, and achievement was based on social recognition of leadership qualities. Leadership was undergirded by material wealth and numerous supporters; kinsmen and followers provided the necessary support for the village headman.

As we have indicated, groups of villages related by agnatic kinship to each other formed a clan, led by a clan chief. Although the clan chief was of the same line of descent as his clansmen, by right of primogeniture he was elevated to the nobility—that is, to a minor noble rank. The higher ranks of the nobility were associated with the princely house and court. The clan had a definite territory in which it pastured its herds and flocks; definite routes of march from one pasture to another; and marks or brands (*tamga*) which were used to identify its herds. The clan was meticulous in its designation of clan members, who were identified by carefully maintained genealogies (there is a steppe saying that every child knows his ancestry to the tenth generation). The clan was equally meticulous in demarcating its pastures and livestock, routes and water sources.

Since clans were political unities, the affairs of the clan were conducted by the chief and the council of elders. They resolved disputes between clansmen and set clan policy regarding other clans, and also transmitted orders to the clan villages and families from the higher leadership, the aforementioned confederation of clans. The confederation was a grouping, loose or firm depending on circumstances: wealth or poverty of the clans; the personal qualities of the leader; amicable conditions within the confederation; threats from abroad. As a rule, it was in the form of a principality under the hegemony of a prince. The clans in the confederation were related; the prince was by this token the senior member of the firstborn line. If antipathies arose between clans, one or another would break away from the parent body and either become independent or—more usually—join another clan and confederation. A new kinship status by the host was granted the group thus joined to a new body, the change being made on application to a higher authority. On joining a new confederation, clans (or villages) were accorded an invented line of descent from a different ancestor than their former one. Fictions of this sort were commonplace on the steppes, and permitted considerable elasticity in the social and political system.

Confederations and princes' reigns were constantly being strengthened or weakened by shifting alliances: fissions and fusions of clans, clan-elements, villages. These movements were motivated by conflicts over pastures, water sources, insufficiencies of fodder and water, diseases of livestock, or incompatibilities between the clans. Whatever the source, the social unit, whether village or clan, felt free to move and find adherence in another place with new social, consanguineal, political, and economic relations.

The clan was the tax unit, providing the princely court with levies of horses, sheep, and wool, and services of postal relays and hospitality to guests and envoys enroute to or from the prince. The clan also provided labor to the prince, his court, and his herds, and troops of horse to the prince's army. The levies, imposts, dues, and tribute-in-kind and in-labor were allocated by the clan chief and council among the villages, to be collected and forwarded by the chief.

Women and Family in the Pastoral World

The woman's world was limited to the tent and to village affairs. Her role may be explained by her life cycle. In childhood, up to the age of puberty, the female was regarded as though she did not exist as a person. For instance, the girl-child was not thought enough of to be barred from adult male ceremonials; her presence simply was not recognized. She could even be given as a chattel in payment of a fine if her father lacked other means of payment. On gaining puberty, however, she finally achieved a definite social status. Marriage arrangements were initiated on her behalf; a marriage portion was set aside for her; the complex set of relationships with her future husband's family and village were now set forth. She no longer belonged wholly to her father's house, but partly, potentially, to her betrothed's. She was no longer a chattel, but had social rights of a limited sort.

The betrothal was arranged by a go-between who was guided by a rule of prohibited degrees of kinship in joining the couple: If they were related in the seventh degree, but not less, sharing an ancestor in the ascending male line in the seventh generation or higher, then they were eligible to marry. The number seven was usual but not universal; its choice was generally associated with a sacred number in the community. The betrothal was affirmed by exchange of gifts and hospitality between the families. The parents of the youth owed respect to the parents of the girl, and her family received payment of "bride-wealth" (usually in livestock) from the family of the youth, or "bride-service" by the youth himself—a period of work in the family of the bride. The bride-wealth was reckoned in livestock, furnishings, and sumptuary goods such as jewels and silks (if the family could afford these). The bride brought her dowry with her, her husband's family thus not only acquiring the services of a potential mother (specifically, a bearer of sons), but in effect getting back a goodly portion of their donation to her. On marriage, the girl's social status rose higher. She had a tent, her dowry, and a menial position in her husband's family, whom she treated with great respect (as she did all the senior males in the household). She addressed them by title—"father-in-law," "husband's elder brother"—and never by name.

If the marriage was fruitful, the girl's position rose even higher: she could not be separated from her children, and maintained tutelary rights over them (in contrast to owing obligations to them). If she was childless, her husband had the power to divorce her by sending her back to her family, but her right to her place in her husband's family was incontrovertible once she had borne a son. The woman who had borne her husband a son achieved full female status, and was a legal person with a complement of rights and responsibilities, with this restriction: she could not administer her husband's property in her own right, but as guardian of her son's right. This body of rights could not be infringed upon. If her husband died, her future status depended on whether she had already borne his family a son. If she was a childless widow, she could be required to pass to her husband's younger brother, a form of marriage known as *levirate*. If she had a son, however, from her first marriage, she was not required to remarry, but could act as guardian of her male offspring and of her deceased husband's estate during the years of her son's minority. If she chose to remarry, her second husband was required to protect the lives and estate of his wife's children by her earlier marriage.

The rights of the type of woman we have been discussing underwent one evolution from the sixth to the eighth centuries A.D., when they were first noted, and have further evolved down to the twentieth. At first a woman had a low status, even if, as we have seen, she bore a son to her husband's line. The Mongol and Turkish mother increased control over her own person and property in the period of 1,400 years during which this development can be traced. The beginning of it is recorded in Turkish writings of the sixth to eighth centuries A.D. in northern Mongolia; the end in reports of the nineteenth and twentieth centuries in various parts of Mongolia and Turkestan. Latterly, among the Kalmuk Mongols of the Volga, and the Kazakhs who are Turks of Central Asia, her legal status has improved even further. By the nineteenth and twentieth centuries the mother had achieved rights as guardian of the property of her son on the death of her husband; and her son asserted a right in the estate of his mother's father. The mother did not yet inherit from her natal line in her own right; this right was—and still is— passed through her to her son.

The slow evolution of women's rights in inheritance, guardianship, and divorce is intertwined with the rise of the state among the nomadic Mongols and Turks. The system of the nomadic state spread over wider territories and embraced ever more peoples and principalities; rights of women increased measurably; and the internal organization of the state became increasingly stable. It would be false to consider these various factors as causes, one of the other. Nevertheless, they were all related in the development of the state on the steppes of Asia, for each factor served to buttress the other.

The Character
of Chingis Khan's Rule

Chingis Khan, whose name in early life was Temüjin, lived from about 1155 to 1227 A.D. He came of a lesser aristocratic descent line. In his young manhood he was often both destitute of supporters and threatened with miserable death, and thus often was in flight. During mid-career his fortunes improved and he gathered about himself a troop of sworn brethren, young men who took an oath of loyalty to his person. By alliance, diplomacy, and force, he gradually extended his domain of command, conquering his rivals on the steppes. In this period, China was suffering from both internal strife and natural disasters: Chinese dynasties were overthrown and the land was divided against itself; and the Yellow River shifted its course, inundating vast areas of the north. For a time, therefore, China was virtually eliminated as a political factor in the steppe. Taking advantage of the situation, Chingis Khan (still Temüjin), after insuring that his Mongol claims were under control, moved into China (and also Turkestan), enriching his domain mainly by raiding.

At some time in the 1190's (at about age 40), Temüjin was renamed Chingis Khan, and was elected leader of the Mongols by his retainers. Some years later he performed the ritual of enthronement before all the people:

> He sent messages to all the peoples in the felt tents and they gathered together in the Year of the Tiger [1206] at the source of the Onon River and raised the white flag with nine tails. They gave Chingis Khan the title Khan there. He appointed Mukhali as *Go-ong*, Royal prince; he commanded Jebe to lead the campaign against King Guchuluk of the Naiman. He appointed leaders of troops of thousands; of the Mongol people, ninety-five leaders of thousands; in addition, he named a leader of the three thousand Onggirat allied to him, of the two thousand Ikires allies, and of the five thousand Onggut and forest people, all of whom he appointed to their posts at that time. The people gathered at the Khan's call, and joined in the ceremonial of his election, the ritual of primary delegation of power to the highest political authority. The ceremony developed further the expression of unity implicit in his call to all the people in the felt tents. The ritual of enthronement, the banner, the appeal to the symbol of the felt tent, all expressed the unity of the people under the Khan.

This account is found in Chapter 8 of the *Secret History*, an official record. It is a prejudiced account, but even then we can see that the people gave their support to the Khan, electing him to his high office and legitimating his claim to rule.

The people were indeed closely bound to the Khan; they fought bravely for the Mongol Empire, rallying to him with high morale. The account in the *Secret History* may be taken at face value: in gathering at the source of the Onon River in 1206, the people expressed their unity under the Khan and ritually acknowledged the mandate which the Khan now possessed to govern over them. This primary act of delegation of the mandate to rule was immediately followed by a secondary act delegating specific powers by the Khan to his chief followers: one was appointed first councillor at the *Ordo*, the Khan's court; another was made field commander; others were given lesser commands.

The traditional religion of the pastoral Turks and Mongols was the same in its general features: they worshiped the great forces of nature—the sky, the earth—which they personified, assigning human attributes to them. They prayed to them, seeking their protection. Their khans took from the heavenly power their mandate to rule over their people. Religious specialists divined the future, interpreting the heavenly dictates for their people from natural and supernatural signs. These individuals, who also were believed to have healing powers, were known as *shamans*; the religion they practiced was *shamanism*. The clans traced their ancestry from mythical beings: Chingis Khan's line as reported in the *Secret History* was descended from the progeny of a wolf and a doe.

Chingis Khan in the early years of his reign continued the practice of shamanism, avowing that in one clan alone should rest the highest priestly office of the empire, because that clan had always provided the shamans for the Mongols. In the conduct of imperial affairs, religious tolerance was practiced: Christians, Moslems, Jews, Confucianists, Taoists, Buddhists, and Shamanists all worshiped side-by-side. The Chinese, Islamic, Buddhist, and Christian religions introduced into the Mongol world some acquaintance with the speculative imagination of the high cultures of Asia and the Mediterranean. They provided a greater play for the spirit and minds of the Mongol court.

With the rise of the empire, the Mongols introduced a new institutional network, the religious. Monasteries, learning, and writings of the great world religions were now widespread in the steppe world. With the collapse of the empire the monasteries were abandoned, and learning and letters shrank in significance. With the later rise of a second Mongol state, however, Buddhism was reintroduced, and with it the monastic centers and the learning and lore of the great faith. Development of their state and empire induced the Mongols to turn their view outward, toward the religion and thought of the world. In the intervening periods, their state formation shrank in size and role, and their view turned inward; contact with world religions and thought was then reduced to a shadow in the dark period of Mongol history, the fifteenth and sixteenth centuries.

Whereas earlier Khans had ruled personally and directly, Chingis Khan ruled through his *nököt*, his personal retinue and company. The earlier khans were close to their people; Chingis Khan governed over them indirectly and reached out to them directly only at the ceremony of his enthronement in 1206. He ruled by delegating his authority, and maintained only formal relations with his people—the exception to this being in his relations to his *nöküt*, whom he forgave even when they committed grievous offenses.

The emperor's edicts (*yasak*) entered and thereby dominated the private family life of the Mongols, as well as their public life. He issued decrees and admonitions regarding such personal matters as distribution of the patrimony among the sons, rights of the children of a concubine in the father's estate, and rights of the son over the wives of the father (other than his mother). One of the purposes of the edicts was to diminish strife within the family and the village. The family and village, by quarreling internally over inheritance, guardianship, orphanage, or divorce, could upset the peace just as thoroughly as would a criminal or mischief-maker. In the interests of imperial harmony, the Mongol emperor sought to avoid disputes within the family. The state increased the magnitude of its responsibilities thereby, while the family was diminished in its degree of autonomy. A consequence of the Khan's rule in this regard was that the family ceased to be an empire within the empire.

Along these same lines, according to an edict of Chingis Khan, women were required to take over all economic matters while the men were away on imperial service. And the wife was also obligated to maintain the hospitality of the household during her husband's absence. This requirement of hospitality was absolute and without reservation. Since particularism emerges out of the question as to who one is, the Tatar polity answers to this criterion; Max Weber classified it as particularistic. The law of hospitality is particularistic. A stranger in a particularistic society must find someone to stand for him and to speak on his behalf. The stranger has no other way of entering the society of the Tatar polity than through his host. Without hospitality, the stranger is a non-person. Membership in the Mongol state depended on a genealogy, and the stranger could not be naturalized save by providing him with a fictional genealogy. If he were to enter Mongol territory and reside there temporarily, the only status, the only protection available to him, was that of hospitality. Indeed, a crime against his person was a crime against the household which afforded him hospitality and protected him.

The center of the Mongol rule was the *Ordo*. Simple in composition at the beginning of the thirteenth century, it was mainly comprised of the emperor's kin, his council, and his *nöküt*. As Mongol power increased there came into the *Ordo* foreign advisers from China, from the settled Turks, from Persia. These were literate ministers who extended the scope of the ruler's knowledge and power, giving him access to information from cultures beyond the steppes.

The empire of Chingis Khan expanded during the first two decades of the thirteenth century into Turkestan, to western and northern China, to the Arab world, to Tibet and India. As new peoples and territories were added, the Khan found it necessary to rule indirectly, through governors who were appointed from among members of his own ruling house, and who regarded the provinces allotted to them as a personal patrimony. The system of rule was consonant with traditional Mongol practice in patrimonial inheritance, extending the family practice into imperial contexts, and it created difficulties in maintaining the central forces of rule. Under Mongol family law, patrimonial rights were bequeathed equally to all the sons, and through them to the grandsons; next, to brothers, father's brothers, and father's brothers' sons. While this system promulgated continuity of family and clan tradition, it was not well suited to needs of rule over all of Asia. China, with its customs, religious creeds, and legal practices, could not be made to conform to Mongol family practice, nor could the Persian or any other polity of a high culture which fell under the Mongol empire.

While Chingis Khan was alive, his armed might, his sense of political and social expediency, the magnitude of his achievements, and his personal qualities all maintained the unity of the empire. On his death, the various provinces his armies had conquered were transformed once more into independent states, principalities, and tribes, and the Mongol rule became transformed into dynasties in Persia, China, Turkestan, Russia, and even the Mongol homeland.

The Mongols, in transforming the political functions of clans and clan-confederations in principalities on the steppes, were able to constitute a state. This state was founded on a society of complex composition, with a hierarchy of classes. Ruling from a central point, the Khan had absolute power of life and death over subjects and kin, sharing this power with none save by explicit and recallable delegation.

European opinion regarded the type of rulership developed in the steppes of Asia as a despotism, an opinion inherited from antiquity and one which continued down to the nineteenth century. Montesquieu, in eighteenth-century France, wrote of the medieval Mongols that they conquered and subdued others only to gratify the ambition of a master. The reason was, he continued, that the people of Tatary, the conquerors of Asia, in fact *were* themselves enslaved.

Montesquieu's view of the Orient was reflected early in the next century by Hegel, who considered that only the monarch was free under the system of the Tatar rule. This thought has its roots in the Greek regard of the Persians in antiquity, for the Greeks considered that their polity permitted great personal freedom and the Persian none, save that of the king. Later European thinkers further promulgated Montesquieu's idea and attached it to the Tatar polity. These dicta should be modified. The Tatar polity was not a despotism of personal whim, but was subject to known laws.

Feudalism
and the Tatar Polity

Some understanding of the Tatar political system can be gained by comparison with the European. The Mongol Empire of the Middle Ages, and comparable Turkish states which together make up the Tatar polity, have been regarded as a feudal form of rule, just as medieval European society and polity were feudal. The application of the feudal theory to Mongolia has been suggested by analogous institutions in both societies. For instance, in both were found the personal retinue of the monarch, and the council of advisers. Also, both societies were divided into estates of noblemen and commoners. Moreover, just as money played only a minor role in the economics of medieval Europe, it did likewise in medieval Tatary: exchange was based chiefly on barter (local produce, grain, farm animals, livestock), and payment of tax and tribute generally was made in barter and/or in labor. Given these conditions, it is not hard to see why, within the village, money was rarely seen, no less exchanged. But of course *some* money was circulated, especially among merchants travelling and trading between Europe and Asia.

In feudal Europe, life was centered around the manor, which was provided for by serfs and dominated by a manor lord. The serfs of a manor were bound to its soil and could not leave without the express permission of their lord. The lord of the manor was in turn pledged in personal fealty to his lord, the king or duke who ruled over the entire territory. But these pledges (among higher-ups) could be denounced if one side or the other failed to live up to its obligations, and thus the knights of Aragon, for example, continued to back up the pledge of their lives to the King of Aragon only so long as he kept them in a condition suitable to their estate. Once the bond was broken, the knights were free to seek another liege lord. Feudal knights were much freer than their counterparts, the Tatar retainers.

In early medieval Europe and in Mongolia, too, towns were few and small and engaged in only limited commercial and administrative activity. Urban life had none of the amenities with which we associate the cities of today; cities of that time were chiefly centers of crafts, markets, fairs, and bazaars— and not yet (as in later centuries) great centers of political power, artistic achievement, learning, or science. Mongolia, as might well be imagined, had severe limitations placed on its urban development.

There also were distinct differences between the Tatar polity and that of feudal Europe. The Mongol society was (in theory, at least) made up of a set of consanguineally related kin groups; although it was divided into social estates, all Mongols—nobility, commoners, and khan—considered each other as kinsmen. This had the consequence of enhancing and deepening the cohesive forces of the society, and of enabling a great degree of social mobility within the political system. The European feudal system was constituted otherwise: the almost unbridgeable social distance between nobility and commoner was such that the European lord was insulted if accused of having "common" blood in his veins. Moreover, the feudal baron was at once private owner and public lord of his domain. As private owner he collected rent from his tenants and as public lord he collected a tax from them, and both monies were deposited in the same purse or treasury. Hence the feudal barons had greater command over their tenants and serfs than did the Tatar nobility.

The Mongol prince in theory at least separated his own herds from those which belonged to the public treasury (his taxes—*alban*—took the form of levies of cattle, horses, sheep, camels, wool, hides, and pelts). Public herdsmen (those subject to tax) were called *albatu*; those in the prince's personal service were called *khamjilga*.

The power of the Mongol Khan was absolute in the sense that all institutions of rule were controlled by him. All areas of public life were immediately dependent on his decrees and edicts, and any personage, no matter how exalted, could be destroyed by withdrawal of his favor. In feudal Europe, however, according to the theory of society then current, the king was constrained from imposing his will according to the legal saying, "The vassal of my vassal is not my vassal." That is, the king, in order to command the services of a tenant belonging to one of his lords or barons, could not do so directly, but had to ask the permission of the manor lord, which indicated that the imposition of commands in Europe differed from the unobstructed power of the Khan. Chingis Khan's realm depended on his decrees and his personal control of the institutions of steppe society and government. The limits to his power were only those inherent in the customs according to which he was raised and which he accepted. Though he ruled through his retinue and *Ordo*, he never had to request permission to do something to, with, or for someone, as did a European local lord or baron of one of his vassals.

The features which Tatars shared with Europeans were (and are) widespread throughout the world. African political systems have the feature of clients of the ruler (those standing in a personal relationship to him, as between master and kinsman)—a different relation from that of subjects to their lord. The council of persons with high rank who advise the king or chief is to be found in various parts of Africa, Polynesia, and America, as well as Europe and Asia. The payment of tax or tribute in produce and in services is characteristic of many non-monetary economies the world over. Since none of these traits is specific to feudal Europe and the Tatars of the Asian steppes, it is not defensible to consider them a single political and social system, namely feudalism.

The development of the political system of the Tatars was uniquely their own, and for this reason has been called the *Tatar polity*. Although it was developed in the Mongol steppes by Turks and Mongols, it was shared with nomadic Turks of Turkey, Turkestan, and southern Siberia, and with Mongol Kalmuks of the Volga, as well as with other nomadic peoples of the central and northern parts of Asia and western China.

Strengths and Weaknesses
of the Tatar State

Government

The political system which formed the backbone of the unique form of state that evolved on the steppes of Asia among nomadic Turks and Mongols has been copied many times and in many places in the world. Many traditional states have borne clan and tribal features; some have carried them into their political constitutions upon becoming complex states. But the social features of the clan and tribe have not been entirely compatible with the requirements of imperial organization: in order to have a durable state, a form of citizenship is necessary which is recognizable and *comparable* throughout the empire; taxation, tribute collection, military organization, administration of justice, foreign policy, postal service, record maintenance, religious service, are needed for government of a complex state and social organization, to meet the requirements of a composite farming, herding, and urban empire. Also, the tax, military, and judiciary functions of the steppe have not always been equal to the enormity of the tasks imposed. Moreover, while the Mongol military technology and battle tactics were superlative, their military organization continued to be based upon the primordial clan-cavalry system of the nomads. The record-keeping was borrowed whole from the Chinese and Persians, while the tax system of the steppe was primitive. The postal service and a policy of religious tolerance were in fact up to the level of imperial demands. Yet achievements of Mongol administration in the different provinces were variable; they were higher in Turkestan than in China, in that they were more smoothly functional and durable. The Mongol polity, which never completely broke with its past, nevertheless underwent an internal development. Although Mongols as individuals were still able to climb (and fall) on their social ladder, the ability to rise was more and more made subject to imperial grace as the social distance between emperor and subject was increased. Whereas the earlier khans had addressed the people directly, the Mongol emperor now spoke through his personal retainers and through the court officialdom. The scope of the emperor's control was extended to internal matters as well as external. He took under his wing private areas of social life, such as family concerns which had been hitherto left to family and village control, beyond the limit of state, public, and official intervention.

The imperial court was functionally divided into administrative areas: civil councilors, religious leaders, military men had separate authorities specifically delegated to them. Governors of outlying provinces had channels of communication distinctive from those of the court functionaries: they did not report through the relevant office, but directly to the emperor.

Social System

Chingis Khan's empire, which appeared to be a unique force to medieval Europeans, was in fact related to foregoing social, political, economic, and military developments in Asia. In the evolution of the state on the Mongolian steppes, the empire of Chingis Khan achieved greater stability in its internal order, greater complexity, and greater geographic extent, than had the realms of the Huns, the Orkhon Turks, and other predecessors. Yet despite differences in scale, the Mongol empire maintained continuity with the Tatar past, and thus was subject to the same limitations, even while entering into a new type of political development.

The Mongol society, as it re-formed, was divided into the royal house and the nobility on the one side, and commoners and slaves on the other. The barrier between commoners and slaves was not great, and was easily breached: by social consent and recognition, by intervention from the throne, by bravery, by special skill such as literacy. Social mobility from the lowest to the highest level was easy, and spanned all levels from the common folk to the royal court.

The clan, a unit of kinship and of political organization, was a building-block of the empire. The clan was the nucleus of civil and military organization. It was the unit of tax collection and provided and equipped troops of horse. The head of a clan ruled over kinsmen; thus the social cohesion of the polity was strengthened. The bond of clanship supported more than the show of political unity: through the spokesmen, the clan directly joined in the election of the prince-chief of the confederation; the clansmen supported him by virtue of the bond which they shared with him, overriding all other considerations.

The social cohesion of the clan and of the principality composed of clan confederations is a stiff and unyielding relationship, and ultimately interferes with regularization of the political order in an empire. The cohesive force of the kinship bond, which supported Turk and Mongol rule among the nomadic peoples, created difficulties in establishing hegemony over farming peoples: the very success of the consanguineal principle, on which social cohesion rested, made its extension beyond the steppe a problem. The basis on which membership in the society could be extended to neighbors sharing a common language, customs, and economy was evident. And even neighbors who differed in language but shared a system of social and political organization and economy could be readily embraced in the empire. These conceptions were the bases on which neighboring Mongols originally and Turks later were incorporated into Chingis Khan's empire. But on what basis could common cause be made with Chinese, Persians, Russians? Thus it was that the lack of viability of the principles of membership in the society and of participation in the polity contributed to the early disintegration of the empire.

The Mongols, on establishing uncontested rule in Mongolia under Chingis Khan, replaced foregoing nomadic pastoral polities in the steppes. Mongolia was a cultural arena in which Turks and Mongols succeeded each other to the supreme power; in this arena the Tatar polity was elaborated from the time of the Huns on.

The clan-and-kin community structure survived both the Mongol Empire and the Tatar state, serving as the characteristic feature of that polity coexisting with the great political enterprises. The clan was applied in new ways—in taxation and in military and religious duties—to the service of the state.

Conservative Forces

The Mongol world retained its limitations, for example, of a society bound together by clan consanguineal relations, and by administrators, such as governors and generals, who were personally bound to the ruler but did not feel so bound to his successor (these individuals ruled territories as personal appanages, and easily removed their holdings from central control, a tendency shared with the Egyptian Empire of the third millennium B.C.).

Because the Mongol Khan was further removed from the people than was the Khan of the Orkhon Turks, the former enjoyed more freedom of action and decision; hence the later rulership was more autocratic, more centralized, and less apt to be swayed by considerations of personality and contingency.

Although this condition is both less humane and less primitive, the development of the state lies neither in the direction of humaneness nor of primitiveness.

Particularism

The Tatar polity was an amalgam of local community practices and institutions characteristic of particularistic societies, and practices of statecraft characteristic of universalistic rule. Chingis Khan governed in part by universal decrees and edicts which affected everyone equally within his empire; in part by making exceptions, allowing for the personal status of this man or that. It is true that modern states also exhibit this amalgam; they attempt to cover the role of personal bonds and loyalties by subterfuges of various kinds. When these are laid bare, then scandal and shame ensue. Chingis Khan, on the other hand, felt no contradiction between the two systems of rule, and was at home in both the particular law of the clan and kin community and the universal law of the state; yet the contradiction was there, even though it was not yet perceived. The practices and institutions of kin community first inhibited the growth of the Tatar state, and then survived it. The modern state, in theory, seeks to overcome the personal bond. However, such a bond was deeply implanted in the Tatar state.

The Place of Women

While women continued to be restricted in peacetime to household affairs and the men to affairs of pasture, hunting-ground, and court, women nevertheless attained more rights and greater public obligations in the course of state formation on the steppes. They became legal persons in a fuller sense than they had been until then, and as legal persons became legally responsible to a greater degree. Rights accrued to them directly during the imperial period, and continued to accrue after the great state enterprise diminished in scope and force. Trends set in motion by the evolution of the early state in regard to personal status were perpetuated even after the specific impetus derived from the state formation, which had brought them about in the first place, went into decline.

Private Rights

Certain rights, such as those of religious worship, just as in China, were guaranteed to all, strangers and citizens alike: respect for all religions was a step toward universalism in the rulership of Chingis Khan. Moreover, taxes and dues were fixed, and the punishment of crimes was explicitly set forth beforehand. The chain of communication to and from the highest authority and the high council was established.

Traditional customs continued in force in public and private law, with the exceptions noted. Such innovations as were made during the reign of Chingis Khan were chiefly those required by the functioning of states in general: in matters such as those of religious tolerance, chain of military command and civil authority, and extension of rights of citizenship by fictional genealogies, the arts of Tatar statecraft were perceived. The heritage of particularism was reflected in the laws of hospitality, in the continuation of the clan system, and in the genealogical basis for confirmation both of membership in society, and of social position.

The development of the Tatar state was a movement in the direction of universalism, and away from particularism. The new factors in the Tatar polity are to be attributed to the universalistic force of the state in administering the law. Their society had until then been composed of a number of self-sufficient and quasi-independent local communities. These local communities were integrated in a state and empire. The extended family and village community continued to function, and the Khan sought to combine them more closely with the state. But the state is not a community of local persons well-known to each other; it is a vast, impersonal body. The administration of justice within the small community takes personal differences into account; the administration of justice in the state tends to be impersonal, its mechanism only occasionally encumbered by personal consideration. On the other hand, justice founded on local custom tends to be fitted to local needs.

The state's justice, although it is mighty and impatient of detail, overlooks individual differences, and may thereby lose meaning to the individual. The administrators of justice in the state, by virtue of their fear of loss of their human identity—or perhaps out of boredom—may act capriciously. The administration of justice in the state, by its very magnitude, may relinquish some of its areas of responsibility to clients and officials who come before it, who are able by reason of wealth or influence to shape the law according to their own interests. In such cases the law of the state takes personal status into account and loses its impersonality. But in general the state tends to move in the direction of universalistic rule, tending to make every law theoretically applicable to one and all.

The Tatar polity, its principles of organization founded on genealogy and personal identity based on genealogy, could not achieve impersonality and impartiality. But it did move in the direction of increasing rights for all, increasing women's rights and obligations correspondingly, and increasing the rights of strangers under the law of hospitality.

Associations

Robert Lowie perceived the germ of the state in the religious secret society of Africa and the military-police association of the Plains Indians. The state as a territorial unity overcomes bonds of local community and kinship by providing alternative associations within the society: association with one's peers, regardless of birthplace or genealogy. While this association is not yet or necessarily the state, nevertheless the processes of state formation are to be seen in the examination of problems which the secret religious orders tend to overcome. States are formed in this way.

Heinrich Schurtz, at the beginning of the twentieth century, and after him Lowie, observed that secret societies are rare among the Turk and Mongol pastoral nomads of central and inner Asia. Having already investigated the processes of state formation in the Tatar polity, among the very peoples from whose ranks the secret societies are absent, we therefore conclude that the state is formed by different peoples independent of each other, in different cultural milieus, and by unrelated processes. The Tatar state had to overcome bonds of local kinship and local community in the process of state formation. The Tatar polity met the same problems posed by Schurtz and Lowie, but in a different way, while evolving a state which in complexity and scope far exceeded the political formation of the Kpelle or Crow.

By retaining the clan and the kin-village, the Tatars inhibited the processes of state development, causing an oscillation between tribalism and state formation. But to the degree that the state was formed, the problems of localism were overcome. The nobility ruled in the clan and clan-confederation and developed bonds outside the local group. The retinue of aristocratic following was transformed into a service nobility in personal bond to the emperor. These institutions of nobility and personal retinue eventually broke through the older network and re-knit the society—although the clan continued to function.

Eventually, after centuries of subjection under the Mongols and Turks, the Chinese, Persian, Russian, and Turkish societies re-formed under new, indigenous leaders, thrust back great numbers of the Tatar nomads, and absorbed or conquered those who remained locally or stood their ground nearby. The Mongols and nomadic Turks, now restricted to their own territories, continued to evolve their small and medium-scale institutions: the kin-village, clan, and clan-confederation, or principality.

The assembly of the entire people was convoked to participate in the primary delegation of social power to the elected emperor. The central authority was thus ritually offered to, accepted by, and imposed upon, the people. The monarch at once appointed personal retainers to offices of limited responsibility. These primary and secondary delegations of power continued to be enacted in the traditional institutional context: the popular assembly and the personal bond between ruler and office-holder. The old institutions had made their mark on the Tatar state formation and limited its development.

Usurpation
and State Formation

Two professors in Russia, W. Radloff and V. Barthold, formed a school in the late-nineteenth and early-twentieth centuries for the study of the languages, history, culture, and society of the Turks and the Mongols. Radloff noted that the pastoral society was composed of families, differentiated by wealth, which were socially unequal. Rich families had great herds, and numerous kin and supporters. Authority in making regulations and arbitrations was vested in personalities outstanding by virtue of descent, wealth, spiritual powers—but above all, by having large followings able to support with deeds or threats the word of their leader. The assertion of authority took place by imposition, and with the support of rich and powerful men of the community, that imposition gained social approval.

Assertion of authority, when backed by force or its threat, which is not based on tradition or precedent, is a usurpation. Gaining control of the grouped villages, the usurper sought to appear as their mandated leader. The union of village communities (*auls*) as an effective instrument of power depended on the personality of the leader. Other families and auls joined the union of the strong leader, supporting him and receiving protection of their interests in the new enlarged community. Such a strong leader founded a descent line that bore his name. Descendants of the original leading family or families in the descent line formed the nobility within the line, enjoying nominal privileges and rights as such. But the nobility had influence only through family wealth and personal capacity.

The descent lines formed clans, which in turn formed by agglomeration clan-confederations. Internal affairs of descent lines or clans were arranged by councils of leaders. A dominant personality could attach to himself increasingly larger numbers of social unities of clans and confederations, in a snowballing effect, and form a great political-military enterprise. Soldiers in the army of such a leader were always available—poor nomads in search of booty. The politico-military enterprise, when it achieved firm contours, was formed into a principality whose leader became by usurpation a self-nominated khan. But most of these khanates were short-lived; the long history of Chingisides was achieved only because the nomads attached themselves to the state formations of the sedentary peoples.

Barthold added that a nomadic people did not ordinarily seek political unity. The individual personality found satisfaction in clan life, without formal agreements or establishment of a highly developed governmental apparatus, without a distinctive executive power and an external coercive force. The khans as expressions of such a state power took the hegemony unto themselves by their own initiative, without having been nominated or elected. The people were faced with an accomplished fact.

The moral order of the nomadic state has never been so severely questioned as it has been by these two experts in its internal structure. Two points are clear in their analyses. (1) The process of differentiating and forming the nobility within the clan as here described is not a theoretical description, but an actual one, among Kazakh nomads near the Sino-Russian border in the nineteenth century. The council of clan leaders in the clan-confederation, and dominance by a forceful personality, actually occurred. (2) The Mongols had no state when they entered Mongolia in the first millennium A.D. They began the process of state formation as they established themselves in that land which had been the scene of state formations by nomadic Turks who had occupied the territory before them.

And yet there can be no thought that a khan achieved his power by usurpation. The Tatars, both Mongols and Turks, had a characteristic internal government, at first weak in conscious and specific elements of rule. Coercive power was dispersed through the society in villages and clans, but it was not concentrated, and hence could not be seized. Gradually, a firm leadership expressed and perpetuated itself.

Usurpation, as we have said, can be applied only if an illegal seizure of power has been made. But the law of the state was not fully developed when the khans first established themselves in power; the state and the khan's position were then in sort of a period of gestation. Hegel showed that a contract was not made to form the state, because the state is the instrument which validates the power of parties to enter into the contract. Just so, a usurpation of power cannot be made in order to form a state because there is no centralized power to usurp until the state has been formed. And it was first formed on the steppes of Asia among the nomad Tatars with the khan at its head. The khan achieved his position in the polity by centralization of the coercive force in the nomadic society. This centralization of force did not precede the state: it was developed in the state and is the mark that the state had been formed.

Chingis Khan proceeded through two stages in the establishment of his power. In the first he gathered his personal following, though his authority was not yet firm. In the second he sent messages to all the nomads and assembled them to witness, participate in, and support his election as Mongol Khan. By their assembly they expressed their consent. There is no sense of usurpation here. Moreover, the state which he ruled after 1206 was a conglomeration of a number of peoples who had never recognized a common ruler before. In the election of the khan by the assembly there is no usurpation; nor is there usurpation in the establishment of a center of power where none had existed before.

But the view of the Tatar state propounded by Radloff and Barthold has a justification. The form of rule was highly personal, depending on the qualities of the ruler as an individual and the loyalty of the *nöküt* in his person. The Tatar-Mongol state partly overcame personal claims to rights of rule, but not entirely. Usurpation is not a just term, but it contains a hint of the personal basis for power which had to be overcome in the formation of the Tatar state.

The Tatar state was developed by internal processes. It is not a conquest state in the sense that one people by physical force gains mastery over another. But there was conquest within steppe society of one group by another. The Turks and Mongols developed their own social order as a society differentiated into high and low estates; at the same time they maintained a system of common descent and kinship. The head of the state was the khan who ruled at first directly; later the khan came to rule through his personal following.

The court of Chingis Khan was a high point in the development of the nomadic state. At its center, the capital city of Karakorum in Mongolia, brilliant feats of architecture and artifice were achieved. Technicians were gathered from Europe and Asia. Ministers from the neighboring agricultural and literate civilizations entered the khan's service, and to these he delegated official powers. He developed his rule by adaptation and re-adaptation of existing institutions. The pledge of personal loyalty as between equals had been the brotherhood of the oath (Mongol: *anda*). This institution of personal loyalty was the foundation of his personal retinue. It was changed in the process from a bond between equals into a bond between master and man. The clan system continued to function in the maintenance of his treasury and army, and in the shamans in his imperial service.

The continuity of the existing institutions sharply constricted the functioning of the nomad state, forcing the ultimate collapse of the empire. The tribal origins of the state were never fully divested by the Tatars while they remained nomads and herdsmen. On the other hand, Turks who took up agriculture developed sedentary states of great stability and duration. The nomadic states, in consequence of their dual consanguineal and territorial operations, were short-lived, unstable, and relatively simple in composition. Nevertheless, this state form briefly held a larger territory in its power than any empire before or since.

The economic development of the nomadic state was at the same time an imperial-political development. Economic and political networks of institutions joined the peoples of China and Mongolia who were specialized as farmers and pastoralists. The pastoralists, as they developed their internal polity in stability and complexity, came as tributaries, raiders, traders, and conquerors to the agricultural civilizations. The integration of peoples with specialized functions in the great institutions was imperfect.

The Tatar nomad state was encumbered by a personal and informal basis of power which limited the permanent institutions. A section of the nobility formed a personal following of the khan. Literate specialists, written records, and the development of the alphabet contributed a modicum of stability and formality to governmental institutions.

By changing internal relations within the society, and by changing external relations, the Tatar form of government was stabilized; thereby the state properly so-called was formed. While stability of the Tatar state depended in part on relations with neighboring farming states and peoples, the state neverthelss was developed by internal processes; the Chinese did not impose by conquest their state upon the Tatars. Turks and Mongols developed their own state by a sequence of primary and secondary delegations of power.

Summary and Conclusions

All societies, stateless or not, have some form of government. The Crow police and military associations; the sacred kingship of Shilluk; the secret society, the kingship, and the master-client relations of Kpelle, all are institutions contributing to the foundation of the state, without themselves forming states. The association and the secret society both have overcome local loyalties, but—at least in the case of Kpelle—have cancelled each other. The productive economy in each case has been lacking in specialized functions; governmental relations were direct and simple; and the kingship and other offices of rulership had little power delegated to them by the people, and thus little to delegate in turn.

Primary and Secondary Delegations of Power in Society

Offices and functions of the state are established through secondary delegation of power by the monarch to his ministers. In Ankole, a stratified society was a system of centralized rule; there was some polarization of power between the king and king's mother and sister. The social force of magic was recognized, resting outside the kingship, supported by the sovereign, and at the same time constituting a factor which the royal power had to deal with. In the case of Kpelle, the alternative pole of power lay in the hands of the head of the Poro, and played no such supportive role. Ankole was an emergent state; Kpelle was not a state at all.

Ankole was more fully developed than Kpelle and constituted an emergent state. Here, herdsmen and farmers lived side-by-side in economically specialized communities; if the farmers were not fully integrated into the military and ritual aspects of the polity, they were nevertheless elements in the economy and in polity as a whole. Ankole government was different in kind from that of Shilluk or Kpelle, but it was different only in degree of complexity of interdependent functions and integration of parts from the governments of Egypt, the Kievan state of Rus, and the Mongol Empire, which were more highly developed states.

Ankole exhibits a *limited* amount of integration of herding and farming peoples; a *limited* amount of popular consensus in the support of the sovereign power; a *limited* degree of differentiation of social function; and a *rigid* stratification by status that inhibits full and free communication. Nevertheless, there was a sovereign power; a modest degree of dispersing that power in specialized offices of rule; and a master-client relation that served to support the kingship and overcome local bonds and loyalties.

The Egyptian state was a fully developed state, with integration of all parts of society—peasants, craftsmen, soldiery, priesthood, and nobility—under one sovereignty, and all geographic localities and provinces in one polity. The art forms and literary formulae show the kingship to have been at once secular and divine, integrating the society under the state. The Slavic polity of Kievan Rus was an early state formed of different parts (peasants, military, nobility, merchants) and of different ethnic groups (Slavs, Norsemen). The Mongol and Turkish nomad states were formed out of personal inheritances (the appanages, and conquests of local rulers), formed with the support of the personal following and retinue of the khan. Just as in the case of Kievan Rus and Ankole, the royal clients and supporters were bound to the person of the king, torn from their places of origin by a new and centralized association. However, the limitation of this kind of bond lay in its personal nature; it did not pass on systematically to the successors or inheritors of the sovereignty—but true states nevertheless were formed which integrated under one power the various social classes and groups. Society, now composed of mutually interdependent parts, was now under one ceiling, the state. The Mongols and their allies gathered to express by a ritual act their unity under the khan. This was at once a primary and secondary delegation of power, just as in Egypt.

The State and the Moral Order

On the question of the morality of the state, Machiavelli propounded the doctrine that the state is subject only to its own moral review. But the state is embedded in its society; it is but one instrument of social control among many, and its acts are subject to the moral judgment and review generally adopted in its society. If the society is complex, its moral system will be complex: there may be more than one moral system in a society.

It is on this moral basis that states, through their representatives, may act on behalf of the body politic—the society in its political aspect. If the body politic feels that its government has offended the prevailing morality, and if an effective counterforce is available, then the government may be voted out or overthrown. If the moral situation still has not been remedied, and if an effective counterforce can be formed, then the state may be overthrown.

If the state is subject to no moral review, it will pose a threat to social morality because of its supreme power. Organs of the state may then force the people to act contrary to the people's moral laws. This is tyranny. Or the state, in a highly complex society with a complex of moral systems, may cause one of these systems to overrule all others. This is dictatorship, and it is dictatorship even if it is that of the majority over the minority.

Corporations may sometimes act as states, under a fiction of sovereignty; but they cannot become states while remaining corporate bodies, otherwise they would be beyond the judgment of the body politic. The ritual of social formation and unification under the state delegates primary power to the central state authority, whereby the state obtains its social sanction. The corporation would negate this condition if it were the state.

Origin or Origins of the State?

The state has not one origin but many. It has originated in independent fashion in various places and at different times. It has arisen in different ways: by external conquest, by internal development, and by both; it has been developed on a territory, and out of combinations of both territorial and consanguineal relationships. The end result, the state, has achieved a unitary form with common features through all its variants; it therefore can be considered in the light of one unitary definition and theory, for it meets problems inherent in ruling large and complex social orders in one way. But the state is only one of several ways whereby mankind has developed a system of ruling large groups of people—both simple and complex societies. Tribal confederations, kingdoms, and leagues, other than the state, have performed the same function. In recent centuries, all but the state have fallen by the wayside.

The study of primitive forms of government and of the state has introduced the factor of population size in the process of state formation. Primitive government is government of a small number of people where everyone knows everyone else. Informal, particularist social controls are invoked under these circumstances. A village leader's judgment is rendered on the basis of his personal acquaintance with the wrongdoer and the innocent, and it is accepted by the community because the chief is known to the people as a person. The larger the number of people in the ethnic group, the less acquainted are individuals; judgments and laws tend to become impersonal. This kind of judgment and legislation is found to an even greater extent in the state.

How large is large in this case? The populations of the Australian or Eskimo bands number in the tens or hundreds. The population of Ankole and of the early Mongol state numbered in the hundreds of thousands. Size of population, in transition from band to state, lies of course between these two sets of figures. But tribes and kingdoms such as Kpelle also number in the hundreds of thousands.

The state is an institution of society, the organ of central rule. It is an institution of whole societies, and not of parts, such as are corporations or other associations, provinces, or communities; and once established it jealously guards its power, sharing it with none.

As an institution of society, the state is submitted to the moral order and judgment of the society. But the state is an institution only of some societies, not of others. It is found in complex societies, serving to integrate the sovereignty over different kinds and classes of people in one supreme office. By its introduction into a social order, the state becomes the integrating factor of society as a secondary social formation—not for the first time, and not as the primary type of social integration.

The state, being the institution of political rule over complex societies, combines under that rule complex and conflicting moral orders. The state on occasion has raised itself to a position of moral neutrality, as arbitrator between the conflicting codes. This has been a means of reifying the state and raising it without justification beyond the reach of moral judgment of the society or societies which it governs. The fact of complexity does not eliminate moral responsibility, but only makes it complex.

There are proponents of the state today who regard it as all-powerful, but we have examined the limitations on the power of the state. There are those who regard the state as existing everywhere in human society, but we have examined forms of the social order in primitive bands and other societies in which the state was absent. Human institutions are limited in power, and are various in form. Familiar solutions to social problems are not the only solutions.

Is the State Found in All or Some Societies?

Anthropologists dealing with the origins and distribution of the state are divided into two camps. On the one hand are those who consider the state to be the organizing principle in all societies. On the other are those who consider that the state has a more limited distribution, to be found only among complex societies as the specialized instrument of rule—that is, as the domination and control of a society by a central office specialized in that role. Among past writers, Eduard Meyer advanced the view of the state as an omnipresent principle of social organization. Elsewhere in his writings he assigned a second meaning, closer to the second usage here expressed, in discussing specifically how the ancient Egyptian state arose. Among more recent writers, W. Koppers regarded the state as universal in human society. Both these men are universalizers in their reference to the state. Lowie, while regarding the state as universal, nevertheless differentiated between the germ of the state in primitive societies and the developed form of the state in complex societies. Religious, territorial, and control features of complex societies governed by states, although they are shared with simple societies, also are changed. Both continuities and discontinuities in human development are applied in the study of the state.

Those who have conceived of the state as existing at all human social and cultural levels have done so by identifying the state with government or politics in general. Certain benefits are incurred by adopting this formulation—above all, the continuity of all forms of human life from the primitive society to the advanced states. Nevertheless, confusion is also introduced: the changing meanings and functions of control, power, ritual, and defense of territory are muddied over unless their application in simple political systems is separated from the state as explicit functions.

The term *government* may be substituted for *state* in the vocabulary of the universalizers. If indeed government is found everywhere in human society, then the term "state" is freed for application in specific social situations—in complex societies with a concentrated source of authority armed with a monopoly of means to enforce that authority. Further, the means of enforcement is one of the specialized functions of the state. The state is the institution which explicitly unifies, defends, and controls a society. Thus the state is seen to be a complicating factor in society. Stateless societies have in an unintegrated way run their internal affairs, defended their territories, and developed and expressed their internal unity. The state, however, performs these functions as the organ of complex societies which is specialized in these tasks. It is the *integrating* regulative and defensive power in those societies in which the state exists. Finally, it performs these tasks for its own sake: those most closely connected with the institution of the state identify the good of society with that of the state. The state becomes an end in itself, and by virtue of its control of physical force becomes the master of the society instead of its servant.

The State
and the Unification of Society

The social unity of the band has a religious ritual expression different from the expression of social unity under the state. Society endowed with a state formation ritually venerates the social unity and the central power which embodies and enforces the social unity. The function of the state ritual is to enforce the unity of the society under the state, to intensify the accord of the people in the rule of the central office.

The ritual of the band expresses its social unity, its sentiment of collectivity, in its common worship and belief; this is the primary process of social unity. Moreover, in the band there is direct participation in the collective ritual. In the state, that unity gains expression in the monarch as ritual leader, high priest, or god-king. Chingis Khan explicitly took unto himself those forces which expressed and maintained social harmony and shared them with no one else.

The records of the early Tatar state, of the state under the princes of Kiev, and that of ancient Egypt all indicate their monopolistic retention both of ritual of power and the reins of authority. These records likewise indicate that ritual was transformed, under the processes of state formation, into expressions of the unity of the society under the state as a secondary process.

The State
and Defense of Society

The territorial unity of the state is different from the territorial unity of the band. The monopoly of power by the central authority is monarchical, whether by inheritance or by election, and is separated from the people over whom it is exerted. The boundaries of the state define not only the limits of the area to be defended from external attack; they define above all the limits within which internal order is maintained by the organs of state power established specifically for that purpose. Firmness of central control and firmness of territorial delimitation are interrelated, as Malinowski has shown.

Primitive bands ward off the intruder because he threatens their economic life, or their existence as a group. The forces of the state ward off intrusive alien powers for these reasons, too; but in addition the state so acts because invasion is both an actual and symbolic infringement of the monopoly of power within its territory, for, under the meaning of the term "sovereignty," the incursions of a foreign intruder diminishes the power of the state.

Because rulers of states have from time to time defined their territorial (and leadership) prerogatives in such a way that the very *idea* of intrusion could cause a war, abstractions such as maps have become a necessary means of defining the bounds of bellicose situations. But territorial rights are but a secondary basis of group or national defense, whereas reasons of economy of effort and group well-being or group security are the primary bases. The indirect, secondary basis of defense is defense for reasons of state: *raison d'état*.

The State
and Control of Society

Application of internal authority in the state is a refinement of techniques common to all societies. Spokesmen for the people delegate primary power to the monarch; this act is adumbrated in the early Egyptian record. Accompanied by popular participation, it is described explicitly in the early Mongol record. But those acts alone did not fulfill the decisive criteria of the state; in each case the monarch had to further delegate his authority. He did this by dividing it among increasingly articulated offices, at the same time (however) retaining the right of veto over the acts of his ministers, and the power to supplant or recall them and to expand or subtract from their functions. One aspect of administration is that of justice. Among the first acts of the princes of Kiev was the explicit assertion of monopolistic right to legally wreak, or cause to be wrought, physical punishment, including the sentence of death.

Maintenance of social control, to which administration of social and legal rules relates, is practiced in the band as well as in the state. The universal presence of means of social control is a mark of unity and continuity of culture. But the techniques of social control, as those of defense of territory, and ritual of social unity, all change function and meaning in the state (as opposed to simple societies).

Lowie has pointed to the origin of the state in those associations which have overcome local kinship and territorial bonds; Malinowski, to the inter-relation of central power in, and precise territorial delimitation of, the state; Morgan, to the significance of the territorial bond in the civil polity or state formation; Steward, to the relation between the complex order of society and the state. Fortes and Evans-Pritchard have contrasted (1) development of an administrative machinery and specialization of governmental functions in the state with (2) government of societies which have none of these attributes. The state achieves the same ends as societies without the state, thus affirming the continuity of human existence, but it does so by different means, thus affirming its discontinuity.

Selected References

Introduction and Chapter One

Bluntschli, J. K., *The Theory of the State* (London: Oxford University Press, 1892). A classic statement of the separation of state and society.

Davis, J. P., *Corporations* (New York: Putnam, 1905). The historical sections and the introduction by Abram Chayes are good background for the treatment of the state and the corporation.

Durkheim, Émile, *Elementary Forms of Religious Life*, tr. by Joseph W. Swain (New York: Humanities, 1915), and *Division of Labor in Society* (New York: Free Press, 1963). Two anthropological classics on religion and the division of labor in society. The latter also treats the question of law and the state.

Engels, F., *The Origin of the Family, Private Property and the State* (various editions). The best socialist statement on the origin of the state by Marx's friend and collaborator.

Ferguson, Adam, *An Essay on the History of Civil Society*, 1767, ed. by D. Forbes (Chicago: Aldine, 1966). Eighteenth-century classic in which the progress (not evolution) of society through the three stages of savagery to barbarism to civilization is first presented.

Fortes, M., and E. E. Evans-Pritchard, eds., *African Political Systems* (London: Oxford University Press, 1940). The concise introduction to the excellent collection of analyses of traditional politics is of especial value.

Fried, M. H., "On the Evolution of Social Stratification and the State," in *Culture in History*, S. Diamond, ed. (New York: Columbia University Press, 1960). An important statement by a scholar presently working on the theory and evolution of the state.

Gierke, Otto, *Natural Law and the Theory of Society* (Boston: Beacon, 1950). Important for coverage of questions of state and morality, natural law doctrine, and theory of the corporate state.

———, *Political Theories of the Middle Age* (Cambridge: Beacon, 1951). Important for the history of the natural law doctrine and the state.

Hobhouse, L. T., G. Wheeler, and M. Ginsberg, *The Material Conditions and Social Institutions of the Simpler Peoples* (New York: Humanities Press). A strict and simple delineation of the problem of social institutions in their relation to material culture in a greater number of societies. Interesting, but outmoded in methodology.

Kelsen, Hans, *General Theory of Law and the State* (New York: Russell, 1961). A statement of law in the state by a neo-Kantian theorist.

Koppers, Wilhelm, *L'Origine de l'État* [Origin of the State]. VI International Congress of Anthropological and Ethnological Sciences, 1960 (Paris, 1963), v. 2, pp. 159–168. The viewpoint is advocated that the state is to be found everywhere in human society.

Laski, H. J., *A Grammar of Politics*, 4th ed. (New York: Humanities, 1957) and *The State in Theory and Practice* (New York: Viking Press, 1935). An Anglo-American theoretician of socialist leanings who contributed importantly to the knowledge of the state, as distinct from governments.

Lowie, R. H., *The Origin of the State* (New York: Russell, 1961). Summary may be found in *The Freeman*, July 19, 1922, and July 26, 1922. Anthropologist of a past generation who developed the theory of the state as formed on the basis of associations. (See MacIver.)

MacIver, R. M., *The Modern State* (London: Oxford University Press, 1926); *Community* (London, 1936). The basic statements of the theory of the state as based on associations.

Meinecke, Friedrich, *Machiavellism* (New Haven: Yale, 1957). Machiavellism and Machiavelli are discussed in terms of the state and morality.

Meyer, Eduard, *Geschichte des Altertums* [History of Antiquity] (1921 and 1925), v. I, pts. 1–2. Also French tr. by A. Moret, *et al.*,

(1914). The basic statement on the universal presence of the state in human society.

Morgan, Lewis Henry, *Ancient Society* (various editions; first ed., 1877). Nineteenth-century anthropologist important for the theory of unilinear human evolution, the state and government included.

Oppenheimer, Franz, *The State* (New York, 1926). Sociological study of the state and the conquest theory of the state.

Radcliffe-Brown, A. R., in M. Fortes and E. E. Evans-Pritchard's *African Political Systems* (London: Oxford University Press, 1940). Preface by Radcliffe-Brown questions the need of the idea of the state in social theory; proposes that government and politics are all that are needed conceptually.

Rousseau, J. J., *The Social Contract* (various editions), Chapter II. One of the eighteenth-century theorists of the theory of the social contract as the basis for human society and the state.

Steward, Julian, *Theory of Culture Change* (Illinois: University of Illinois, 1955). Develops theory of multilinear evolution—the state formed in several places independently.

Thurnwald, Richard, *Die Menschliche Gesellschaft* [Human Society], v. 4 [The State] (Berlin-Leipzig, 1935). Important restatement of the theory of the formation of the state by conquest, particularly with reference to East Africa.

Vinogradoff, Paul, "Outlines of Historical Jurisprudence," v. 1., in Lawrence Krader's *Anthropology and Early Law* (New York: Basic Books, 1967). Classic historical scholarship in the line of Maitland. Discusses Roman and medieval law, the family, society, kinship, and the state.

Weber, Max, *Essays in Sociology*, ed. by H. H. Gerth and C. W. Mills (New York: Oxford University Press, 1946). Basic discussion of state functions—economy, bureaucracy, law, in social context.

White, Leslie, *The Evolution of Culture* (New York: McGraw-Hill, 1959). Argues for theory of unilinear evolution of society and the state in the line of Morgan's researches.

Chapter Two

Elkin, A. P., *The Australian Aborigines* (New York: Doubleday, 1964). Includes passages on government without the state in Australian societies.

Evans-Pritchard, E. E., "The Divine Kingship of the Shilluk of the Nilotic Sudan," in *Essays in Social Anthropology* (New York: Free Press, 1963). Important depiction of a simple government with a symbolic form of kingship without state power.

Hoebel, E. A., *The Law of Primitive Man* (Cambridge: Harvard University Press, 1954). Includes description of Eskimo law and government.

Lowie, R., *The Origin of the State* (New York: Russell, 1961). Government of the Crow Indians based on associations of military as contributing to state formation.

Morgan, Lewis Henry, *Ancient Society* (various editions). See above, comment in Introduction. Includes data on Iroquois government without the state.

Quain, B. H., with W. Fenton, "The Iroquois," in M. Mead's *Cooperation and Competition Among Primitive Peoples* (New York: Beacon, rev. ed., 1961). Includes research since Morgan's day on the Iroquois.

Westermann, D., *Die Kpelle* (Göttingen, 1921). Kingship described as midway between the symbolic form (see Evans-Pritchard, *Shilluk*, above) and the more highly developed and actually ruling king of Ankole (see Chapter Three).

Chapter Three

Fortes, M., and E. E. Evans-Pritchard, *African Political Systems* (London: Oxford University Press, 1940).

Oberg, K., "The Kingdom of Ankole in Uganda," in M. Fortes and E. E. Evans-Pritchard's *African Political Systems*. Basic description of Ankole kingship and polity.

Thurnwald, Richard, *Die Menschliche Gesellschaft* [Human Society], v. 4 [The State] (Berlin-Leipzig, 1935). Critique of the conquest theory of the state.

Chapter Four

Frankfort, Henri, *Kingship and the Gods* (Chicago: University of Chicago, 1948). A study of ancient Near Eastern religion as the integration of society and nature.

Frankfort, Henri, *et al.*, *Intellectual Adventure of Ancient Man* (Chicago: University of Chicago, 1946); also *Before Philosophy* (Penguin). Important for early Near Eastern data on the formation of the state in ancient Egypt, with Mesopotamian comparisons.

Meyer, Eduard, *Geschichte des Altertums* [History of Antiquity] (1921 and 1925), v. I, pts. 1–2. (See comments above.) Basic description of the rise of the Egyptian state.

Moret, Alexandre, and G. Davy, *From Tribe to Empire*, tr. by V. Gordon Childe (1926). Contains a sound picture of the formation of the Egyptian state. Follows ideas of Durkheim (see above) and Eduard Meyer.

Chapter Five

Dvornik, Francis, *Slavs in European History and Civilization* (New Brunswick: Rutgers University Press, 1962). General description of ancient and medieval Slavic life and culture.

Grekov, B. D., *Kiev Russia* (Moscow and San Francisco, 1959). Rise of the state in ancient and medieval Russia.

Hensel, Withold, *The Beginnings of the Polish State* (Warsaw, 1960). Rise of the state in ancient and medieval Poland.

Marquart, Joseph, *Osteuropäische und Ostasiatische Streifzüge* [East European and East Asian Excursions] (Leipzig, 1901). Comparative work on society and culture in Eastern Europe and Asia in the Middle Ages.

Niederle, Lubor, *Manuel de l'Antiquité Slav* [Manual of Slavic Antiquity] v. 2. (Paris, 1926). Somewhat outmoded, but still sound on formation of Slavic states in ancient and medieval times.

Chapter Six

Barthold, V. V., *Four Studies on the History of Central Asia*, 3 vols. (New York: W. S. Heinman Imported Books) and *Turkestan Down to the Mongol Invasion* (London, 1928). A great scholar's works on the empire of the Chingis Khan and the succession states that emerged out of the empire.

Harmatta, Janos, *The Dissolution of the Hun Empire*, Acta Archaeologica (1952, v. 2, no. 7, pp. 277–304. The rise and fall of an early Tatar state. Contains a critique of the theory of the Tatar state developed by Barthold and Radloff.

Krader, Lawrence, *Social Organizations of the Mongol-Turkic Pastoral Nomads* (New York: Humanities and The Hague, 1963). *Peoples of Central Asia* (Indiana, Uralic and Altaic Series, 1963). Social anthropological and social historical accounts of the political systems of the Turks of Central Asia and Mongols of Inner Asia, including government, rise of the state, and law.

Marquart, Joseph, *Osteuropäische und Ostasiatische Streifzüge* [East European and East Asian Excursions] (Leipzig, 1901). (See above under Chapter Five).

Conclusions—See Introduction and Chapter One.

Index